How Does God Do That?

Complete Earth Science with an Introduction to Life Science
Ages 8 - 12

Paul and Danielle Harris

Coffee House Publishers

How Does God Do That?
Paul and Danielle Harris

Coffee House Publishers
32370 SE Judd Rd
Eagle Creek, Oregon 97022
503.637.3277
roadsearching.com

Cover design: Durand Demlow
Interior Design: Demlow Design
Illustrations: Paul Harris

This book was created with QuarkXpress 3.3 on Macintosh and Motorola computers. The fonts used were Palatino and Bookman.

ISBN
987654321

For Donald Miller

Thank you for bringing us together.

The authors wish to express gratitude to Shirley Bjur who, just before press deadline, helped make last minute adjustments.

Special thanks to Elsa Harris who was patient with her parents during the year-and-a-half process of writing this book.

About The Authors

Paul and Danielle Harris both earned degrees from George Fox University in Newberg, Oregon. Paul holds a Bachelor of Science degree in Biology and a Master of Arts in Teaching. Danielle, this book's principal author, owns a Bachelor of Arts degree in Writing and Literature and a Master of Arts in Teaching. Today they live in Hermiston, Oregon where Paul teaches mathamatics and coaches both basketball and baseball. Danielle stays home to raise their daughter Elsa. In addition to being actively involved in the community, Paul and Danielle serve as youth leaders at Hermiston Christian Center. As this book goes to press, they are expecting their second child.

TABLE OF CONTENTS

A Note to Parents

THE PURPOSE OF THIS BOOK: My husband and I are both educators and parents. As educators in the secular school system, we know the frustration of being limited in how much we can point to God as the creator of the universe. Thus, as parents of a one-year-old toddler and a soon-to-be-born baby, we are strongly considering homeschooling our children so that they will not be limited by the school system in which they learn. As educators, we know what we want from a science book — something that is simple, straightforward, and easy to follow. We want a book that allows us to provide enrichment where we wish, but does not require us to translate everything into "plain English" so the student can understand. As parents, we also know what we want from a science book — one that continually points to God's awesome power, creativity, and artistry. As we considered these two desires, we recognized the need for a God-centered, but teacher-friendly, science book and endeavored to create it in *How Does God Do That?*

CHILD RESPONSIBILITY: The book is designed to take responsibility from you, the teacher, and place the responsibility on the student. We wrote this book directly to the student, and used a character named Captain Explorer to transport your student all over the universe--from the ends of our galaxy to the cells in our bodies. We believe that one of God's greatest inventions is the imagination, and we encourage the student to stretch this God-given gift often in this science book.

PARENTAL INVOLVEMENT: Though this book is written directly to the student, there are many ways in which the parents can be involved in the student's discovery of science. Students can use the review questions at the end of each chapter to quiz Mom or Dad and correct any wrong answers. Perhaps the explorations of your student and Captain Explorer can be a discussion topic at the dinner table, beginning with the question, "Where did you and

Captain Explorer visit today?" As teachers, we have come to understand that the best way to learn a subject is to teach it. The more ways in which the parent can act as the student, and the student as the teacher, the more ways in which the student's understanding will be increased.

There are other ways in which you can be involved in the science education of your child. Before starting the book, it is important to know how the book is organized. Look over the table of contents with the student. We have chosen to visit the vast parts of the universe first, and the minuscule parts of our bodies last. (For younger students, this can be described as simply going from learning about big things to little things.) We visit the universe and our solar system in Unit 1, explore planet Earth in Unit 2, and cover the details (God's handiwork) on Earth in Unit 3. Earth science is completely discussed, and a good introduction to life science is covered in this arrangement.

STUDENT OBJECTIVES: Each chapter begins with student objectives. This long list of what the student will do can be overwhelming. Rather than having the student read this entire list, we recommend a different approach. As the teacher, skim the amount of material to be covered for that day, and write (or have the student write) the student objectives to be completed for that day at the top of a piece of paper. This gives the student a few goals that can be checked off when completed. Not only will you be encouraging your student to measure his or her own success, but you will also be teaching important study and life skills. Perhaps you know the difference a "to-do" list can make in organizing your day and helping you see all you have accomplished. Teaching this skill at this early age will be extremely beneficial in the entire education and life of your child.

SCRIPTURES: We have attempted to integrate scriptures throughout the book. However, the significance of these scriptures will probably be lost if you do not discuss them with the student. The introduction of each chapter is meant to help the student focus on God's amazing design in the universe. Though we have attempted to capture enthusiasm with the written word, nothing can match a teacher's enthusiasm that is almost always contagious, even with the more reluctant students. We recommend that you read the introduction together, spend time in discussing God's amazing universe, and prepare the child to anticipate what will be discussed. In teacher language, this is called the "anticipatory set." If you capture the student's interest here, you are almost guaranteed a great deal of learning. On the other hand, if you lose the student at this point, learning is bound to be a struggle.

ACTIVITIES: As we mentioned before, as teachers, we wrote this book to be teacher-friendly. Almost all the activities require no special materials, no teacher-intensive preparation, and very little explanation. The activities are straightforward and simple, yet help the student to review concepts that are discussed in a variety of ways. As educators, we know that there is a push to develop activities that integrate other subjects with science. We have attempted to include many integrated assignments in this book.

Many times, the student is asked to complete charts and graphs in the book. This is an attempt to get the student to see the "whole picture" rather than memorize isolated scientific facts. In order to create, complete, or even understand a diagram or chart, students must synthesize most of the information covered in that section. We believe that by often putting the focus on the chart or diagram, students will be encouraged to see the main points of the section and understand how they relate to each other.

THE METRIC SYSTEM: Because the academically accepted standard of measurement is the metric system, we have chosen to follow this standard. Before you and your student begin reading this book, it is very important that your student knows the units of the metric system and how to translate these measurements into something they understand. For younger students, it will be important to have a meter stick and a ruler on hand, so they can see the actual distances of these units of measurements in concrete form whenever they come across them. For older students, you should begin by teaching how to translate kilometers, meters, and centimeters into miles, yards, and inches. A good activity might be to create a chart with these translations and tape it on the inside cover of the book, so the student can refer to it whenever he or she wishes.

It is also important to discuss the differences between Celsius and Fahrenheit. For younger students, it is probably enough to recognize that water boils at 100 degrees Celsius (212 degrees Fahrenheit), and water freezes at 0 degrees Celsius (32 degrees Fahrenheit). Older students are probably ready to use the conversion formula, which can also be taped to the inside cover of this book.

REVIEW QUESTIONS: Though we boast about this book being teacher-friendly, there is one area which is bound to be teacher-intensive. At the end of every chapter, there is a review. These review questions were designed to be very different from what is commonly used in science books. Rather than the review section being a time of choosing the correct multiple-choice answer, we worded questions in a way that would encourage the student to better his or her understanding of the information studied, as well as better his or her study skills.

Review questions will encourage students to look back in the chapter for answers. After tutoring students individually, we have found that this skill is something that must be taught. Students do not do this naturally, especially when there are choices in front of them which they can choose from without turning a page. Questions also encourage students to summarize information and put this information into their own words. This skill is vitally important. The ability to put information into words from the student's vocabulary not only helps his writing and verbal skills, but also reveals his understanding of what is being written, rather than his ability to recite what has been written. There is a very large chasm between a student's recitation of information and actual understanding of information.

These reviews will probably be a struggle for you and your student at first. Please, be patient. It is likely that your student has not been asked to do more than one or two questions per chapter in which he actually had to formulate his own, original answers. It will take time for him to become accomplished at this skill. We encourage you to spend time in teaching him how to restate the question in the answer. This helps the student to focus on what information is needed. It is also important to work with your student in learning how to recognize what is being asked. Teaching him to focus on the verbs such as "list," "compare," "identify," etc. will help him not only with this science book, but with all subjects.

EVOLUTION: In the secular school system, science books fail to even recognize creationism as a viable theory. Throughout any secular science book, evolutionism is the basis of the book and is not treated as a theory, but mentioned in passing as undeniable fact. Likewise, in this book, we do not discuss evolutionism. Creationism is the basis of the book and is not treated as a theory, but mentioned in passing as undeniable fact. At this age, we feel that the focus should be on God and his works. As students mature, evolutionism should be discussed. Many good books that show the differences between evolutionism and creationism are available when the time is appropriate.

WORDS OF ENCOURAGEMENT: We understand the challenges of teaching. We know both the highs of student excitement in learning, and the lows of student lack of motivation or desire. We designed this book to be a tool for you to encourage both you, as a teacher, and your student, as a learner. As you travel through the universe with your child, we hope this fresh approach to science will help you and your child to focus on the wonders of learning and the joys of discovery. Bon voyage!

God's Vast Creation

One

1

Hello! My name is Captain Explorer. I am gathering a crew to explore God's universe. Our mission is to discover how God designed our world and beyond it. To be a part of this adventure, you have to sign up as one of the crew. If you would like to join, sign you name here.

Signature:_____

As your captain, I will be assigning certain duties to you, and you will be expected to perform them quickly, thoroughly, and neatly. Some of these duties will include:

searching for information

performing experiments

creating or completing illustrations, charts, and tables

composing paragraphs

Our first trip will be to a very important star. Can you guess which star it is? Write your guess on the line below and then turn the page. _____

Chapter 1: Our Solar System
Student Objectives

My objectives are:

1. I will illustrate how the sun is special to me in a drawing.

2. I will create a model or a drawing of the sun and label its parts.

3. I will tell time by the sun.

4. I will list the materials which make up the sun.

5. I will draw and write about an imaginary journey to another planet in our solar system.

6. I will identify the inner, minor, and outer planets.

7. I will create a chart of the planets in our solar system and describe each planet's main characteristics.

8. I will demonstrate how the sun affects Earth's days and nights and its revolution through activities.

9. I will complete an illustration of the earth and its relationship to the sun and moon.

10. I will list the days of the week in order.

11. I will list the months of the year in order.

12. I will list the holidays of each month.

13. I will define diameter, period of rotation, period of revolution, orbit, greenhouse effect, retrograde motion, hydrosphere, magnetosphere, superheated water, and double planet.

14. I will compare the diameters of Mercury and Jupiter in a math activity.

15. I will label the main parts of a comet.

16. I will compare a meteorite, meteoroid, and meteor.

Chapter 1: Our Solar System

In this first part of the journey, we will travel very far—millions of miles. We will visit our very own sun! Did you know that the sun is actually a star? It is a star that is similar to the millions of other stars you see in the sky. Yet, our sun is different in at least one very big way—we could not live without it! We need the sun for light. We also need the sun for heat and food. The sun is the main source of energy for living things. To us, the sun is special. God designed this star to be especially suited to us. Psalm 19:4-6 says, *". . . He has set a tabernacle for the sun, which is like a bridegroom coming out of his chamber, and rejoices like a strong man to run its race. Its rising is from one end of heaven, and its circuit to the other end; and there is nothing hidden from its heat."* The sun should show us the thoughtfulness and mightiness of our Creator. Take a moment to praise God for designing this special star. Afterwards, in the space below, draw a picture that shows one way the sun is special to us.

Very good! Let's learn more about this special star.

OUR SOLAR SYSTEM

Section 1-1: The Sun

How big is it? It is so big that, if the sun were hollow, over one million earths could fit inside it. However, the sun is just a medium-sized star compared with others!

What are the sun's main characteristics? The sun is made of very hot gases. The gases that make up the sun are always in motion, so the surface of the sun seems to be uneven.

Four main layers make up the sun's atmosphere. Planets and moons can have atmospheres too. An atmosphere is a mixture of gases that surround a star, planet, or moon. These are the four main layers in our special star, the sun:

CORONA: The outer layer of the sun's atmosphere is called the corona. This layer surrounds the sun like a halo. Gases in this layer can reach temperatures up to 1,700,000 degrees Celsius. (Note that water boils at 100 degrees Celsius!)

CHROMOSPHERE: The middle layer of the sun's atmosphere is called the chromosphere. The chromosphere gives off a faint red light that we cannot see, because the other layers of the sun are too bright. It is several thousand kilometers thick. Temperatures average 27,800 degrees Celsius.

PHOTOSPHERE: The photosphere is the outermost layer of the sun's atmosphere. This thin layer of gas gives off a brilliant light, which is the part of the sun that we see every day. It is 550 kilometers thick, and the temperature does not usually rise above 6,000 degrees Celsius.

CORE: The sun's center is called the core. This is the hottest part of the sun. At its outer edges, temperatures may reach 1,000,000 degrees Celsius, but near its very center, temperatures may reach 15,000,000 degrees Celsius.

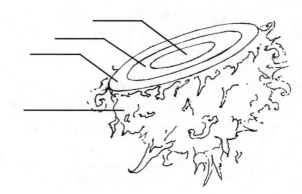

Label the layers of the sun.

Activity: Re-create the Sun!

If you don't have access to clay, try drawing a cross-section of the sun, using the illustration on the previous page, and markers or colored pencils to show the different layers.

Materials: Four colors of clay, rolling pin, toothpicks, glue, paper, pen, or pencil, butter knife, scissors

Procedure:
1. Roll clay of one color into a ball about one inch thick. This will be the core of the sun.

2. Using another color, pat the clay out until it is flat. Then, take the rolling pin and roll the clay out until it is very thin. Wrap it around the core. This is the photosphere.

3. Using another color, pat a large amount of clay out until it is flat, but thicker than the color you used for the photos phere. Wrap it around the photosphere. This is the chromos phere.

4. Using another color, roll out a very thin layer to cover the other layers. This will be the sun's surface.

5. Cut an edge off the ball so that all the layers can be seen.

6. Draw four small boxes on a piece of paper. Inside the boxes, write the names of the four layers and the temperature of each layer.

7. Cut out the boxes and glue them to the toothpicks.

8. Put the toothpicks into the correct layers on the model.

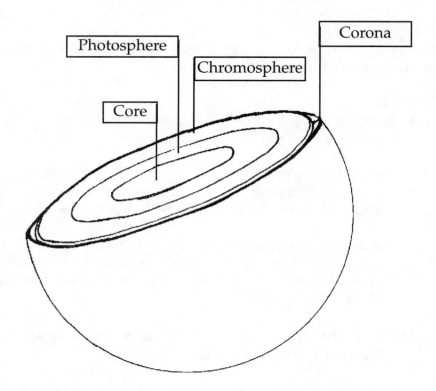

You created a model of the sun! A **model** is an object that represents something else. Since we cannot bring the actual sun into our classroom to study, we create a model of the sun.

Good work, mate.

Activity: Tell Time by the Sun

Materials: 3 foot wooden stake, a stick of something which will mark the ground

Procedure:

1. Find a place where the sun shines from noon throughout the day.

2. A little before noon, place the stake so that a shadow is cast on the ground.

3. Mark the edge of the noon shadow.

4. At every hour after, mark the edge of the shadow.

5. Over the next few days, tell time by the shadow, estimating when the shadow is between markings. Then, check the actual time using a watch or clock. Record your results.

Date	Your Time	Actual Time

Good job! We've made a long journey to the sun, yet our journey has just begun. We will continue through our entire solar system. Our solar system includes the sun, the planets, and all the other objects that revolve around the sun, and we will visit them all!

Section 1-2: The Planets

Journal activity: Imagine you are visiting one of the planets in our solar system. Draw what you see and write a paragraph that describes your experience. Then, as you read, check to see if your imagination is correct.

_____

_____

_____

_____

_____

_____

_____

Nice job! You have completed another assignment successfully!

When looking at nature, it is easy to see that God has designed it. Look at a flower, the bark of a tree, or a bird and you will see God's perfect handiwork, from the smallest to the biggest creation. Yet God's handiwork doesn't stop here on earth. His work extends far beyond our little planet, Earth. He created the millions of stars, which we have used for navigation and farming. He created planets, asteroids, comets, and meteors, all of which we can study and be amazed at God's vast creation!

However, our little planet, Earth, is the only one in our solar system that contains life. If we were closer to the sun, it would be too hot for us to live. If we were farther away from the sun, it would be too cold. God placed us in the perfect position away from the sun so we could live. Let's visit the other planets and see how different they are from Earth. Each planet that we will visit is unique and interesting. As we travel to each planet, think about the mighty God who created this vast universe.

As you read the paragraph below, try to fill in the parts that you know. As you read the section, fill in the spaces you missed and correct the wrong guesses.

The solar system is divided into two parts: the **inner planets** and **outer planets**. The inner planets are the four planets that are closest to the sun. They include _____, _____, _____, and _____. They outer planets are the five planets that are farthest from the sun. They include _____, _____, _____, _____, and _____. Dividing these two groups are the **minor planets**. Can you guess what these are? Put your guess on the line below.

_____

On the next page, you will see a chart that is
not finished. Your job is to complete the chart.
Read the instructions below to help you fill in
the information correctly.

First column — Name each planet in the first column, beginning with the planet that is closest to the sun and ending
with the planet that is farthest from the sun. We will be visiting the planets in this order, so if you fill in your answers
as we go, you should be able to fill in the rows from top to
bottom.

Second column — List how far the planet is from the sun in
kilometers.

Third column — List the planet's diameter in kilometers.
The **diameter** of an object is its width.

Fourth column — In terms of earth-days and earth-years, list
the planet's **period of revolution**, or how long it takes for a
planet to revolve around the sun. A planet's period of
revolution is called a year on that planet. For example,
Mercury — the planet closest to the sun — takes about 88
earth-days to revolve once around the sun. So a year on
Mercury is about 88 earth-days long. Pluto — normally the
planet most distant from the sun — takes about 248 earth-
years to revolve around the sun. So a year on Pluto is about
248 earth-years long. Now, in giving these two examples,
I've also given you two answers to fill in on your charts!

Fifth column — List the planet's **period of rotation**, or the
time it takes for a planet to spin once around. While the
planet is moving around the sun, it is also rotating on its

axis, an imaginary line through the center of the planet around which the planet spins. The earth takes about 24 hours to rotate once on its axis. Does that number seem familiar? There are 24 hours in an earth-day. The time it takes a planet to go through one period of rotation is called a day on the planet.

Mercury takes almost 59 earth-days to rotate once on its axis. A day on Mercury, then, is almost 59 earth-days long. Pluto takes just over six earth-days to rotate once on its axis.

So a day on Pluto is a little more than six earth-days long. Once again, your captain has given you answers for your charts. Take the time to fill those in now!

Sixth column — List the number of moons each planet has.

Seventh column — As you read the information scroll on each planet, pick out one interesting aspect of the planet and write it in this section.

 **Chart of the Planets**

Planet Data Chart						
Planet name	Km from sun	Diameter in km	Revolution period	Rotation period	Number of moons	Interesting aspect

Are you ready to continue our journey? The first planet that we'll visit is the planet that is closest to the sun—Mercury. Mercury is the sun's nearest neighbor, just 58 million kilometers from the sun. Mercury is the first of the inner planets. (Hint: Remember to fill in the section on the previous page, as well as your chart.) The planet is named for the Roman messenger god who was very quick. Mercury moves around the sun faster than any other planet. Turn the page and read the information scroll on this interesting place.

Mercury

How big is it? Mercury is not much bigger than our moon. It is 4,880 kilometers in diameter.

How many moons does it have? Mercury doesn't have any moons.

What are some of its main characteristics? Mercury's surface is covered by craters. Mercury appears to have many giant curving cliffs that extend hundreds of kilometers, cutting across its craters. Some of them are as high as 3 kilometers.

What is its climate like? Because it is the planet closest to the sun, Mercury has no atmosphere to shield it against the heat of the sun or the cold of space. Remember, a day on Mercury lasts 59 earth-days. Because the planet rotates so slowly, the surface gets very hot on the sunny side and very cold on the dark side. Temperatures rise to more than 700 degrees Celsius on the side that is facing the sun. On the side that is night, the temperature drops to about -200 degrees Celsius.

Imagine if, instead of lasting 24 hours, our day lasted 58 days. Our planet would be much hotter and colder as well. However, God designed our Earth to rotate fast enough so that neither side would get too hot or too cold. Isn't that amazing?

Did you know? Because Mercury is the closest planet to the sun, the rising sun appears nine times as large as the sun does on earth.

Also, a year on Mercury lasts only 88 earth-days. That's less than three months. Imagine if our year was less than three months. The seasons would change so quickly, our plants and animals wouldn't know what to do. Hibernating animals would just get to sleep when they would have to be awakened again. God designed our planet to rotate in the perfect amount of time.

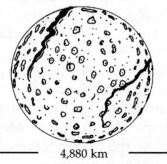

4,880 km

Now we will travel to the next inner planet —Venus. Venus is 108 million kilometers away from the sun. It is covered by thick clouds, so for many years, scientists were uncertain about the surface of Venus. Many people imagined Venus might be covered with vast oceans and tropical forests.

Venus

How big is it? Venus is 12,104 kilometers in diameter, which is very close to Earth's diameter. In fact, Venus is often called Earth's twin sister planet.

How many moons does it have? Venus doesn't have any moons.

What are some of its main characteristics? The surface of Venus is constantly covered with thick clouds made mostly of sulfuric acid. Because of the thick cloud cover, it has been difficult to study the Venusian surface. The data that has been gathered has shown that Venus has many craters on its surface, as well as vast plains and tall mountains. There is some evidence that volcanoes once erupted on Venus. There is also a giant crack in the surface that is much deeper and longer than Earth's Grand Canyon.

Did you know? The sun rises in the west and sets in the east on Venus. Why? Because Venus rotates on its axis from east to west. So while most of the other planets are rotating in the same direction, Venus is going the other way. This backward rotation is called **retrograde motion**.

Also, a day on Venus is longer than a year! It takes about 243 earth-days to complete one period of rotation (a Venus day), and it takes 224 earth days to revolve once around the sun (a Venus year).

12,104 km

God used such variety in creating the planets. Each one is unique and has its own interesting aspects. Now, let's go to our own planet, the wonderful planet Earth! When we reach Earth, we will have traveled 150 million kilometers from the sun. It was once believed that Earth was the center of the universe, and that the sun revolved around our planet. However, God designed our Earth to be part of a balanced system--nine planets revolving around our special star, the sun. God created Earth to be the most unique and special planet, the one that contains life. Before we learn about our special planet, let's test you to see how much you already know.

Earth Test

How big is the planet earth?

What is its period of revolution (how long is a year)?

What is its period of rotation (how long is a day)?

How many moons does it have?

What is the temperature high?

What is the temperature low?

What makes up its atmosphere?

What are some of its main characteristics?

As you learn about our planet, check your answers and
correct any incorrect answers.

Earth

How big is it? Earth is 12,756 kilometers in diameter, just slightly bigger than its sister planet, Venus. Compared to Jupiter, which has a diameter of 142,800 kilometers, Earth may not seem big, yet it is the largest of the inner planets, the four planets nearest the sun.

The distance around the earth, called its circumference, is 40,000 kilometers. This line around the earth's fattest part is called the equator. Can you guess what color the equator is? Put your guess on the line below. Then check to see if your answer is in the following copy.

_____

The equator divides the earth into two parts, the Northern Hemisphere and the Southern Hemisphere. Find which hemisphere you live in and write it on the line below.

_____

How long is a day (period of rotation) and year (period of revolution) on earth in earth time? A day is 23 hours, 56 minutes, 4.09 seconds, and a year is 365 days, 6 hours, 9 minutes, 9.54 seconds!

Some vital statistics: The earth has one moon. Can you imagine what it would be like to live on Saturn, which has 23 moons? The temperature high on earth is 58 degrees Celsius at Al Aziziyah, Libya; and the temperature low is -90 degrees Celsius at Vostok in Antarctica.

Which gases make up Earth's atmosphere? The oxygen you breathe makes up about 21 percent of the earth's atmosphere. About 78 percent of the atmosphere is nitrogen. The rest is made up of gases such as argon, carbon dioxide, water vapor, hydrogen, helium, neon, krypton, xenon, and methane.

What are some of the main characteristics of Earth? Earth has life! There is water to drink, air to breathe, food to eat, and plants and trees to grow. Earth is our home! Looking at earth from a distance, one of its notable features is the earth's rocky crust which varies in thickness. Beneath the oceans, the crust may be only eight kilometers thick. Beneath the continents, the crust may be 32 kilometers thick.

Another notable feature is that 70 percent of earth's surface is covered by water. This water is called the **hydrosphere** and includes the earth's oceans, rivers and streams, ponds and lakes, seas and bays, and the water frozen in the icebergs, glaciers, and polar ice caps at the North and South Poles.

What color is the equator? Trick question! The equator doesn't have a color. The equator is an imaginary line around the earth.

**Take this time to correct your Earth test
and fill in your planetary chart.**

Earth's Days, Months, and Seasons

We learned that the planets revolve around the sun. However, in earlier times, people imagined that the sun and moon revolved around the Earth and that the earth stood still. God set the sun and the planets in their places and has ordered their movements ever since. In Genesis 8:22, God promises us that the earth's movements are in his control -- While the earth remains, seedtime and harvest, and cold and heat, and winter and summer, and day and night shall not cease.

Earth has two movements. Like the other planets, Earth spins on its axis as it travels around the sun. Remember that the earth's axis is an imaginary line from the North Pole through the center of the earth to the South Pole. These two movements of the earth -- the spinning on its axis (rotation) and the traveling around the sun (revolution) -- affect both day and night and the seasons on Earth. Let's learn more about how the earth's movements affect our days, months, and seasons.

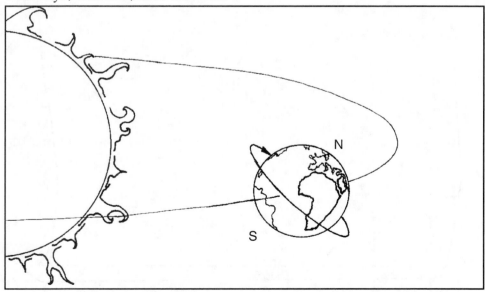

Day and Night

It takes Earth about 24 hours to rotate once on its axis. The amount of time Earth takes to complete one rotation is called a day. Thus, a day on Earth is about 24 hours long.

As the earth rotates, part of it faces the sun and is bathed in sunlight. It is daytime for this part of the Earth. The rest of the earth faces away from the sun and is in darkness. It is nighttime for that part of the earth. As the earth rotates, the part that faced the sun soon disappears into darkness. The part that was in darkness comes into sunlight.

Imagine that you are looking down on Earth from above the North Pole. You would see that the earth rotates in a counterclockwise direction, or from west to east. As the earth turns toward the sun, it appears to us that the sun is rising in the east. As the earth turns away from the sun, it appears to us that the sun is going down or setting in the west.

You may have noticed that during the summer, we have more daylight than in the winter. That is because the earth's axis is tilted at a 23-1/2 degree angle. If the earth's axis were exactly straight up and down, all parts of the earth would have 12 hours of daylight and 12 hours of darkness every day of the year. Because of the earth's tilted axis, when the North Pole is leaning toward the sun, the South Pole is leaning away from the sun; and when the South Pole is leaning toward the sun, the North Pole is leaning away from the sun. The hemisphere that leans toward the sun has long days and short nights. The hemisphere that leans away from the sun has short days and long nights.

Period of Rotation Activity
(Day and Night)

Materials: Globe, flashlight and sticker

Procedure:
1. On the globe, place a sticker on the region where you live.

2. Rotate the globe once. This represents one 24-hour period.

3. Darken the room and shine the flashlight on the globe.

4. Turn the globe so that your home is facing the light. This is similar to the Earth's position during your day. Notice that the other side is not lighted. On the other side of the Earth, it is night.

5. Rotate the globe slowly to see how the sun orders our nights and days.

Questions:
1. Does the sun ever turn off?

2. When the flashlight shone on the sticker, was it day or night?

3. As the globe turned, what happened to the sticker?

4. What causes day and night?

Day and Night Illustration

Materials: Crayons or colored pencils and paper

Procedure:
1. Connect the two dots at N & S poles with a black line to represent the Earth's axis.

2. Draw an orange sun on the right side of the Earth.

3. Draw a yellow moon on the left side of the Earth.

4. Color the side that is near the sun green. It is daytime for this side.

5. Color the side away from the sun dark blue. It is night for this side.

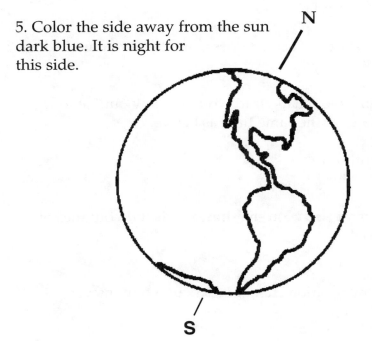

Activity: Tracing Your Shadow

Materials: Sunshine and chalk

Procedure:

1. On a sunny day, have someone trace your entire shadow on a sidewalk or concrete slab. (Be sure the entire shadow is traced, including the outline of each student's feet.)

2. Write your name, the day of the week, and the time on the inside of your outline.

3. Discuss the possibility of whether your shadow outline will change if you stand in the exact position and at the same time four to five days later.

4. Write a hypothesis, or educated guess, of whether your shadow outline will change.

5. Using a different color chalk, trace your shadow outline four to five days later at the same time as before.

6. Compare the outlines.

Questions:

1. How many days passed between drawing the two outlines of your shadow?

2. Did your shadow position change? Explain your answer.

The Seasons

We just learned on the previous page that Earth's axis is tilted toward the sun for part of the year and away from the sun for part of the year. (Look at the figure below.) When the Northern Hemisphere is tilted toward the sun, it is summer for that hemisphere. When it is summer for the Northern Hemisphere, it is winter for the Southern Hemisphere which is tilted away from the sun. The hemisphere that is tilted toward the sun receives more direct sunlight and also has longer days as we learned on the previous page. This causes the hemisphere to receive more heat from the sun, resulting in the summer season.

The longest day of the year occurs on what is called the **summer solstice**. This is the day when the North Pole is tilted a full 23-1/2 degrees toward the sun. For the Northern Hemisphere, this occurs on June 20 or 21 and is the first day of summer. The word solstice comes from two Latin words meaning "sun" and "stop." It refers to the time when the sun seems to stop moving higher in the sky each day. The sun reaches its highest point in the sky on the summer solstice.

For those who live in the Northern Hemisphere, the sun will appear to move lower and lower in the sky until December 21 or 22, when the **winter solstice** occurs. At this time, the North Pole is tilted a full 23-1/2 degrees away from the sun.

Twice a year, in spring and autumn, neither the North Pole nor the South Pole is tilted toward the sun. These times are known as equinoxes. The word equinox comes from Latin and means "equal night". At the equinoxes, day and night are of equal length all over the world. In the Northern Hemisphere, spring begins on the vernal equinox, March 20 or 21. Autumn begins on the autumnal equinox, September 22 or 23.

Period of Revolution Activity
(Year)

Materials: Flashlight, orange, and two toothpicks

Procedure:

1. Insert a toothpick at opposite sides of the orange, representing a planet's axis.

2. Darken the room and turn on the flashlight.

3. Tilt the orange slightly on its axis, so the bottom half points toward the lamp. This is summer for the bottom half, and winter for the top half.

4. Walk around the room, keeping the orange in the same position. On the other side of the room, the bottom of the orange should be pointing away from the light. This is winter for the bottom half, and summer for the top half.

Note: As you walk around the light, you are representing a planet's **orbit**. The path that planets and moons follow in their travels is called an orbit. An orbit is roughly circular. The Earth and the other planets travel in an orbit around the sun. Moons orbit around the planets.

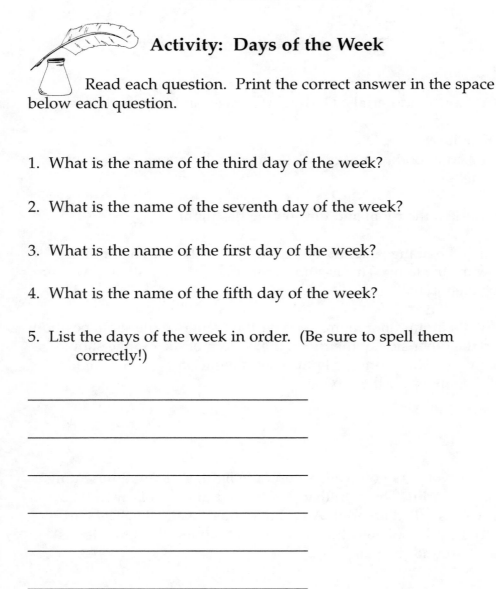

Activity: Days of the Week

Read each question. Print the correct answer in the space below each question.

1. What is the name of the third day of the week?

2. What is the name of the seventh day of the week?

3. What is the name of the first day of the week?

4. What is the name of the fifth day of the week?

5. List the days of the week in order. (Be sure to spell them correctly!)

_____

_____

_____

_____

_____

_____

Activity: Months of the Year

Using a calendar, answer the questions below.

1. If this month is April, then last month was _____.

2. If next month will be November, then this month is _____.

3. If this month is April, then next month will be _____.

4. If next month will be July, then this month is_____.

5. If last month was July, then this month is _____.

6. If last month was June, then this month is _____.

7. If this month is January, then last month was_____.

8. If next month will be May, then this month is _____.

9. If last month was January, then this month will be _____.

10. If this month is October, then next month will be _____.

11. If next month will be February, then this month is _____.

12. If last month was August, then this month is_____.

Activity: Exploring a Calendar

Materials: Calendar(s)

Using your calendar, answer the following questions:

1. The calendar represents one year. How many months are in one year?

2. One row on the calendar represents one week. How many days are in one week?

3. How many weeks are in one month?

4. Which months have 31 days?

5. Which months have 30 days?

6. Which month has 28 days (sometimes 29)?

7. On which days could you see a full moon?

Activity: Holidays

Using a current calendar, find the months in which these holidays occur. (Not all of the months will be named. Some months may be named more than once.)

1. New Year's Day _____.

2. Christmas _____.

3. Valentine's Day _____.

4. Thanksgiving _____.

5. St. Patrick's Day _____.

6. Presidents Day _____.

7. Groundhogs Day _____.

8. Father's Day _____.

9. Labor Day _____.

10. Memorial Day _____.

11. Easter _____.

12. Independence Day _____.

13. Mother's Day _____.

14. Martin Luther King, Jr. Day _____.

Now we will leave Earth and travel to the last of the inner planets. Mars is 228 million kilometers from the sun. Mars is named after the Greek god of war. Its red color gives the planet a bloody appearance. The two tiny moons that orbit Mars also have warlike names: Phobos and Deimos, which mean "fear" and "terror." Why is this planet red? Read the answer to *Did you know?* and you'll find out!

Mars

How big is it? Mars is 6,794 kilometers in diameter. That's a little more than half the size of Earth.

How long is Mars' period of rotation and revolution? Mars' rotation and revolution is very similar to Earth's. A day is 24.5 hours, and a year is 1.88 earth years.

What is the climate like? Mars is a cold and windy planet. Its temperature high is about -31 degrees Celsius, and its low is -130 degrees Celsius (earth's low is -90 degrees Celsius). Windstorms sweep across the surface at speeds of up to 200 kilometers per hour, stirring up dust.

The planet has water on it, but it is all frozen. Frozen water can be found in the northern ice cap and under the Martian soil. The southern ice cap of Mars is made of frozen carbon dioxide.

What are some of its main characteristics? Mars has four huge volcanoes. Though vast lava plains hint that these volcanoes were once active, they are now dormant. The largest volcano on Mars is Olympus Mons. This volcano is wider than the island of Hawaii and almost three times as tall as Mt. Everest. It is the largest known volcano in the solar system.

Another interesting feature of Mars is an enormous canyon called Valles Marineries. The canyon is 240 kilometers wide at one point and 6.5 kilometers deep. If this canyon were on earth, it would stretch from California to New York.

Did you know? Martian soil is mostly made of a chemical called iron oxide, otherwise known to us as rust! This is the reason for its red color. Mars is a rusty planet. When the winds of Mars sweep up this red dust, the sky turns a dark pink.

Let's review our journey. We have just finished visiting the **inner planets**. These planets include: Mercury, Venus, Earth and Mars. Our next part of the journey will be dangerous. We will visit the **minor planets**. We must pass through thousands and thousands of rocks and "flying mountains," which are known as the **asteroid belt**. The asteroid belt sweeps around the sun between the orbits of Mars and Jupiter.

Asteroids are made of metals, rock, or a combination of the two. A few of the asteroids are massive. For example, Ceres, the largest asteroid, has a diameter of almost 1,000 kilometers. Most of the asteroids, however, are small.

Color the illustration on the next page of our ship dodging the asteroids.

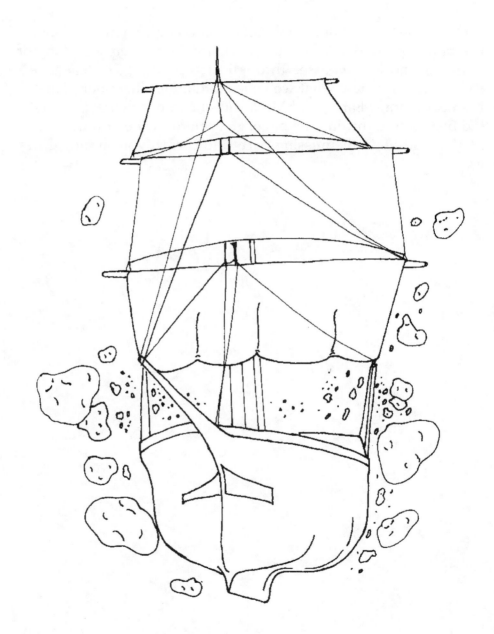

Excellent! While you've been completing the illustration, Captain Explorer has been busy dodging these interesting "minor planets," and we've passed through successfully. Now let's take some time to review what we've learned about the inner planets, Mercury, Venus, Earth, and Mars, and the minor planets, the asteroid belt. Before turning the page, go back to the beginning of the section and fill in the missing parts and correct your wrong guesses.

Now we begin our journey to the outer planets. Four of these five planets are called "gas giants," massive planets made primarily of gases. Jupiter, the largest planet in our solar system, looms ahead. This gas giant is 142,790 kilometers in diameter. Jupiter appears so big and bright to us on earth that the Romans named this planet after their king of the gods.

This planet is like our sun in many ways. It is mostly made of hydrogen and helium gases. At the center of Jupiter, scientists believe temperatures may each 30,000 degrees Celsius, which is almost five times the temperature of the surface of the sun! Scientists believe that Jupiter could have almost been a star when it was formed, but God had a different design for our solar system.

As we near Jupiter, 779 million kilometers away from the sun, all that we can see of the planet's atmosphere is its thick cloud cover. These clouds appear as swirls and bands of color. The clouds are very active. Let's learn more about this huge planet.

Relative distance of the planets from the sun. Note how much farther out the outer planets are.

61

Jupiter

How big is it? A hundred earths could be strung around Jupiter. Its diameter is 142,700 kilometers wide.

What is its period of rotation and revolution? A day on Jupiter lasts about 10 hours. A year lasts about 11.86 earth years.

How many moons does it have? Jupiter has 16 moons. The first bodies in the solar system to be discovered by telescope were the four large moons of Jupiter, observed by Galileo in 1610. He discovered and named Io, Europa, Ganymede, and Calisto, after four lovers of the Roman god Jupiter.

What are Jupiter's main characteristics? Jupiter has huge storms that whirl across its surface. These storms can be seen because the colored bands of clouds are twisted and turned by the strong winds. Perhaps the best-known feature of Jupiter is the Great Red Spot. This giant red spot has been observed for over 300 years and is believed by scientists to be a huge hurricane. The Great Red Spot is three times as big as earth and, if it is a storm, it is the longest storm every observed in the solar system. Can you imagine what it would be like to be at the center of such a storm?

From space, we can observe Jupiter's thick cloud cover, but we must guess about the rest of the planet. Scientists believe that Jupiter has only a small solid core surrounded by a giant ocean of liquid hydrogen. The clouds nearest the core are thick and dense. Because of the thick cloud cover, the atmospheric pressure on Jupiter is enormous.

Did you know? Jupiter is unique in many ways. Jupiter has a giant magnetic field called the **magnetosphere** which is caused by the atmospheric pressure. This magnetosphere stretches for millions of kilometers beyond the planet and is the largest single structure in the solar system. Jupiter is also unusual in that it give off more heat than it receives. Jupiter is so hot that it radiates about 1.5 times as much energy as it receives from the sun. Remember, scientists believe that Jupiter could have been a star.

Activity: Math

Comparing Diameters: Jupiter, the largest planet in our solar system, has a diameter of 142,800 kilometers. Pluto, the smallest planet in our solar system, has a diameter of 2,274 kilometers. How many more kilometers is Jupiter's diameter? Write your answer here. _____

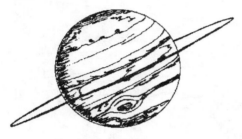

Jupiter's Diameter
142,800 km

Pluto's Diameter
2,274 km

Now it is time to leave Jupiter and to journey to another gas giant in the solar system — Saturn! When we reach Saturn, we will be 1,427 million kilometers away from the sun. Saturn is the second largest planet in the solar system. It has a diameter of 120,000 kilometers.

As we have learned so far, there is something unique and amazing about each and every planet. As we near Saturn, the first thing we will notice is its magnificent rings. Saturn's rings were first discovered by Galileo, and it was the first planet found to have rings.

The rings of Saturn are made mainly of icy particles. Saturn appears to have three main rings when observed from earth. However, photographs taken by spacecraft show that Saturn has at least seven major rings, lettered from A to G. The outer edge of the most distant ring is almost 300,000 kilometers from Saturn.

Relative distance of the planets from the sun

Saturn

What are some of Saturn's main characteristics? Like Jupiter, Saturn is made mainly of hydrogen and helium gases. Because Saturn spins so fast on its axis, it is flattened at the poles, and it bulges at the equator. Like Jupiter, Saturn's clouds form colored bands around the planet. There is even an orange oval in Saturn's southern hemisphere, a smaller version of Jupiter's Great Red Spot.

What is its period of rotation and revolution? A day on Saturn lasts about 10.5 hours. A year lasts about 29.46 earth years.

How many moons does it have? Saturn has more moons than any other planet and astronomers are still coming. Scientists believe there are 23 moons. The largest moon of Saturn is Titan. It has a substantial atmosphere made of a combination of gases that gives it a hazy orange glow.

What is its climate like? Also like Jupiter, the planet has violent storms. One enormous lightning storm detected by astronomers lasted for more than two months. Near the equator, a superfast jet-stream, four times as quick as the fastest winds of

Jupiter, speeds around the planet at about 1,800 kilometers pre hour. Saturn is colder than Jupiter, yet it gives off three times more energy than it gets from the sun. Saturn also has a huge magnetos-phere.

Did you know? Saturn is the least dense of all the planets. If there were an ocean big enough to hold Saturn, it would float!

We have come a long way, almost 1.5 billion miles, and yet our traveling has just begun. Uranus, the seventh planet, is now our destination. This planet is twice as far from the sun as Saturn. The orbit of Uranus is 2.8 billion kilometers away from the sun. Saturn is only 1,427 million kilometers away from the sun.

Uranus was named for the father of Saturn. Like Jupiter and Saturn, it is also a gas giant. Also like the other gas giants, Uranus is covered by a thick atmosphere. However, Uranus' clouds do not have bands. The entire planet is a greenish-blue color.

Uranus

How big is it? Uranus is 50,800 kilometers circimference.

What are some of the planet's main characteristics? Uranus has a rocky core about the size of earth. The entire planet is covered by an ocean of **superheated water** that is about 8,000 kilometers deep. Superheated water is water that is heated past its boiling point, but it does not evaporate into steam. It stays in liquid form because of the extremely high atmospheric pressure on Uranus.

How many moons does it have? Uranus has 15 moons. Two of these moons are named Miranda and Ariel, both of which are geologically active.

What is its period of revolution and rotation? A year on Uranus is 84.6 earth years. A day is approximately 16.8 hours.

Did you know? Uranus rotates at about a 90-degree angle, which means it rotates on its side. The 11 rings of Uranus also surround the planet from top to bottom, rather than circling the planet horizontally. Unlike the rings of Saturn, the rings of Uranus are dark and probably made of methane ice.

Color the picture below of Uranus and draw its nine rings. Note the color of the planet on the previous page.

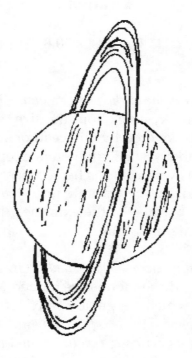

Nicely done! Now we are going to visit what has been called Uranus' twin giant — Neptune. Neptune and Uranus are about the same size, mass, and temperature. Neptune also glows with a blue-green color. Like Uranus, Neptune is covered by a thick cloud cover, and temperatures for both planets may dip to a chilly -220 degrees Celsius.

Neptune was named for the Roman god of the sea. It is 4.5 billion kilometers away from the sun.

Neptune

How big is it? Neptune is 48,600 kilometers in diameter.

What are some of its main characteristics? Neptune's surface is probably an ocean of water and liquid methane, covering a rocky core.

How many moons does it have? Neptune has at least eight moons. The most interesting moon is Triton, the fourth largest moon in the solar system. Triton has an atmosphere, and appears to be covered with frozen methane. Triton is unusual in that it orbits Neptune in a backward, or retrograde, direction.

What is its period of rotation and revolution? Neptune's day lasts 18.5 hours, and its year lasts 164.5 earth years!

Did you know? Neptune has five rings made of dust particles. It also has an unusual satellite rotation. At certain times, it is further from the sun than Pluto.

Neptune is very similar to Uranus in
size, density, color, and its two rings.

We will now journey to the last planet discovered in our
solar system. Pluto is named for the Roman god of the underworld. This planet is the furthest (5.9 billion kilometers) away
from the sun, and it is the tiniest planet, only 3,000 kilometers in
diameter. Mercury, the small and quick inner planet, is over
twice the size of Pluto. Turn the page to learn more about Pluto.

Pluto

What are some of the planet's main characteristics?
Scientists believe that Pluto is made of various ices,
mostly of methane. On the sunny side of Pluto, the
ice may have evaporated to form a thin, pink atmosphere. On the dark side of Pluto, the ice is frozen. If
this is true, Pluto is the only planet in our solar system that has half an atmosphere — one on the sunny
side, and none on the dark side.

What is its period of rotation and revolution? A
day on Pluto lasts six earth days and 9.5 hours. A
year lasts 247.7 earth years!

How many moons does it have? Read the *Did you
know?* and you'll find out!

Did you know? In 1978, astronomer James
Christy discovered that Pluto a moon. He named the
moon Charon, after the mythological boatman who
ferried the souls of the dead into the underworld.
Charon is about half the size of Pluto. Because of this
closeness in size, astronomers consider Pluto and
Charon to be a **double planet**. That means the two
planets revolve around each other, rather than a
moon revolving around a planet.

OUR SOLAR SYSTEM

Now it is time to complete your chart of the planets, the fill-in-the-blank part at the beginning of Section 1-2, and the definitions below. When you are finished, turn the page and we'll learn more about space!

magnetosphere:

superheated water:

double planet:

diameter:

period of revolution:

period of rotation:

orbit:

greenhouse effect:

retrograde motion:

hydrosphere:

Our Solar System

Section 1-3: Comets and Meteors

Comets

We have traveled to the sun, past the inner planets, past the asteroid belt, past the gas, giants and Pluto, and now we will blaze our own space trail beyond the solar system into a vast collection of ice, gas and dust some 15 trillion kilometers from the sun! We will visit the Oort Cloud, named for the Dutch astronomer, Jan Oort.

Every once in awhile, the gravitational pull of a nearby star will tug a mountain-sized "dirty snowball" out of the Oort Cloud and send it speeding toward the sun. This is commonly called a comet. As the **comet** nears the sun, some of its ice, gas, and dust heat up enough to form a cloud around its core. The core of a comet is called its **nucleus**. The cloud around the nucleus is called the **coma**. A solar wind from the sun blows the coma away from the sun to form the comet's **tail**. Label the nucleus, the coma, and the tail in the illustration below. Notice that the tail always blows away from the sun.

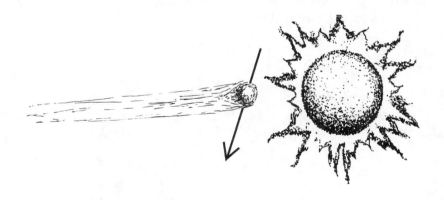

Most of the 100,000 comets or so orbit the sun again and again. These comets are divided into two types: **long-period** and **short-period** comets. Long-period comets may take thousands of years to sweep past the earth once again. Short-period comets, however, return to the sun every few years. One of the most famous of these is Halley's Comet, named for the English astronomer, Edmund Halley. Halley was the first to realize that the comets seen in 1456, 1531, 1607, and 1682 were really the same comet. Halley predicted that the comet would return again in 1759, but he died without knowing if he was right. He was! The last time Halley's Comet was seen was in 1986. We should see it again around 2062. How old will you be when Halley's Comet sweeps past earth again? To figure this out, subtract the date of your birth from the number 2062, and write your age on the line below.

_____

Wow! You could be a grandma or a grandpa when Halley's Comet comes to visit again!

Meteoroids, Meteors, and Meteorites

Have you ever been watching the sky when a "shooting star" dives across the sky? Many people make wishes whenever they see a shooting star. However, most people don't know that shooting stars aren't stars at all. They are actually **meteors**. Meteors are created by **meteoroids**, which are chunks of metal or stone that orbit the sun. Each day the earth is invaded by millions of meteoroids. When the meteoroid rubs against the gases in the atmosphere, friction causes it to burn. The streak of light produced by a burning meteoroid is called a meteor.

Most meteors burn up in the atmosphere. A few strike Earth's surface, however. A meteor that strikes Earth's surface is called a **meteorite**. While most meteorites are small, a few are quite large. The largest meteorite ever found is the Hoba West meteorite in southwest Africa. It has a mass of more then 18,00 0 kilograms.

In the United States, the enormous Barringer Meteorite Crater, between Flagstaff and Winslow in Arizona, is the most famous.

Write the correct term for the definitions in the spaces below.

meteorite

meteoroid

meteor

_____: a chunk of metal or stone that orbits the earth

_____: a meteoroid that is burning

_____: a meteor that strikes the Earth's surface

Excellent work, mate!

Chapter 1 Review

1. What is the definition of **atmosphere**?

2. Of which materials is the sun made?

3. Name the four main layers of the sun.
    a.

    b.

    c.

    d.

4. Which layer of the sun is the brightest? (Which layer is the part of the sun that we see every day?) Which layer of the sun is the hottest?

5. What is a **model**?

6. List the four inner planets and the five outer planets.

7. What are the minor planets?

8. Which planet(s) travel in a retrograde or backward rotation?

9. In a paragraph, describe some of the main characteristics of Earth.

10. Why does Mars appear red?

11. Which is the smallest planet? Which is the largest?

12. What term is used to describe four of the five outer planets?

13. Which planet is known for its spectacular rings?

14. Which planets are called the twin giants?

15. Which planet is considered by astronomers to be a double planet?

16. Describe the Oort Cloud.

17. What are the differences between long-term and short-term comets?

18. When a chunk of metal or stone from outer space strikes the Earth's surface, what is it called?

Student Objectives
Chapter 2: Beyond Our Solar System

My objectives are:

1. I will compare the different sizes, temperatures and colors of stars.

2. I will complete an illustration of a constellation and identify it.

3. I will create my own constellation.

4. I will define multiple-star system, binary stars, composition, and constellation.

5. I will compare the different types of galaxies.

6. I will define galaxy.

Chapter 2 — Beyond Our Solar System

He counts the numbers of the stars. He gives names to all of them.
Psalms 147:2-3

Section 2-1: Stars and Constellations

During our exploration of the universe, we visited our own special star, the sun. However, the sun is just one of millions, perhaps billions, perhaps trillions of other stars! God's universe is so huge that we have a difficult time understanding it. The more we understand of God's creation, the more amazing it seems!

We have left our own solar system behind, and now we will travel to the star that is nearest to the sun, Alpha Centauri. Even though this star is the closest to the sun, it is still 4.3 light years away. The speed of light is about 300,000 kilometers per second. If we were to travel at the speed of light, it would take about 4.3 years to reach the sun's nearest star. Don't worry, we will travel at a much faster rate than that!

As we near this star, you will notice that Alpha Centauri is actually a group of three stars revolving around each other--a triple star system. When more than one star revolve around each other, it is called a **multiple-star system**. Viewed from Earth, these multiple-star systems appear as a single speck in the sky. However, astronomers have discovered that about half the stars in the sky have at least one companion star. Most of these stars are double-star systems in which two stars revolve around each other. Double-star systems are called **binary stars**.

After visiting Alpha Centauri, we will turn to a star that is almost 400 light years from Earth. I'm sure you have heard of the

North Star, or Polaris. Polaris has been an important star to navigators at sea because they knew if they steered toward Polaris they were heading north. This point brings us to one of the reasons why God placed the stars in the sky. Over the centuries, people have used the stars for navigation. Think of some other ways we have used the stars. In the past, people watched the stars to know when it was time to plant their crops. They have also watched the stars for signs. In the Bible, the magi followed a star to Jesus. Let's move on to learn more about stars.

Characteristics of Stars

Size: Astronomers have divided stars into five main groups by size. The smallest stars of all are called **neutron stars**. A typical neutron star has a diameter of only about 16 kilometers. You probably travel this distance every day. **White dwarfs** are bigger than neutron stars, but some may not be any bigger than Earth. The smallest known white dwarf, Van Maanen's star, has a diameter that is less than the distance across the continent of Asia.

Medium-sized stars make up the majority of the stars you can see in the sky. They vary in size from about one-tenth the size of the sun to about ten times its size. So, our sun fits in the medium-sized category. Many of these stars are very bright. Sirius, for example, is a medium-sized star and is the brightest star in the night sky.

Stars with diameters about 10 to 100 times as large as the sun are called **giant stars**. Even the giant stars, however, seem tiny in comparison to the largest of the stars. **Supergiant stars** have diameters up to 1,000 times the diameter of the sun. If a supergiant were to replace our sun, it would extend beyond Mars and burn Earth to cinder. These stars are, however, the shortest-lived stars in the universe.

Use the corresponding letter to identify the star with its description. Then color the illustration below, and go to the next page to learn more about the characteristics of stars.

_____ giant star

_____ neutron stars

_____ medium-sized stars

_____ supergiant stars

_____ white dwarf stars

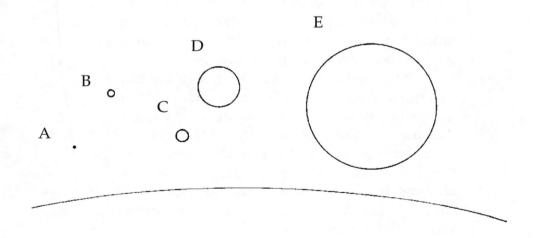

Composition: Astronomers have discovered that almost all stars are made of the same things, or have the same composition. Hydrogen, the lightest element, is the most common element in a typical star. Helium, the second lightest element, is the second most common element. Hydrogen and helium together make up about 96 to 99 percent of a star's mass. Other elements often include oxygen, neon, carbon, and nitrogen and make up a little more than four percent of the star's mass.

Surface temperature and color: The color of a star is one of the best clues for astronomers to decide how hot it is. The hottest stars shine with a blue or blue-white flame. Surface temperatures of these stars can reach 35,000 degrees Celsius. The next hottest color is white, with a surface temperature of 10,000 degrees Celsius. Yellow-colored stars, such as our own sun, have a surface temperature of 6,000 degrees Celsius. Cooler stars have a red-orange color. These stars have a surface temperature of about 5,000 degrees Celsius. The coolest star of all is a red color, with a surface temperature of about 3,000 degrees Celsius.

The chart below needs to be completed. Fill in the chart with the missing information.

Color/Heat Chart	
Color	**Temperature**
blue	
	10,000 °C

Constellations

Polaris, or the North Star, is at the end of the handle of a group of stars called the Little Dipper. The Little Dipper is part of a **constellation** called Ursa Minor, or the Little Bear. Constellations are groups of stars in which people at one time saw imaginary figures of animals and people.

A constellation that is probably familiar to you is Ursa Major, or the Big Bear. The seven stars on the back and tail of the Big Bear form the Big Dipper. On clear winter nights, other constellations you can see are Orion the Hunter, Gemini, Canis Major, or the Big Dog, and Canis Minor, or the Little Dog. Some of the summer constellations that are easy to see are Scorpius, Leo, and Virgo. Look at the figure below. Circle the constellation that you know.

Activity:

On a starry night, go outside and draw a section of the sky with all of its stars. Afterwards, connect the stars to create your own constellation. It can be an animal or person, or something that is modern or from the past.

Section 2-2: Galaxies

Let's continue our journey out into the vast expanses of space. In 1914, American astronomer Harlow Shapley began studying large groups of stars. Shapley discovered that the groups of stars were clustered together in a gigantic sphere. Most of the stars that were known in Shapley's time were in a part of the sky called the Milky Way. The Greek name of the Milky Way is galaxies kylos, which means milky circle. Shapley's universe came to be called a **galaxy**. Shapley believed that all the matter in the universe was located in this single galaxy. Outside the galaxy there was empty space.

In 1755, long before Shapley was born, the German philosopher-scientist Immanuel Kant suggested that there were other "island universes," or galaxies, scattered throughout space as well.

Who was right? We have traveled beyond our own solar system, beyond many different stars and constellations, and now we will pass out of our own galaxy. Will there be nothing but empty space as Shapley believed? Or will there be many vast galaxies to visit? We do not have to travel far to see the answer. Surrounding us are many "island universes" of various shapes and sizes. Kant was correct! Even though the Milky Way is 100,000 light years from one end to the other, it is but one tiny galaxy in a sea of galaxies. God's creation seems to go on forever, and who knows? Perhaps it does.

As we speed out into space, we begin to see a pattern in the shapes of the galaxies. Many galaxies are **spiral galaxies**. Spiral galaxies have huge spiral arms that seem to reach out into space. Our own Milky Way is an example of a spiral galaxy. Other galaxies are nearly spherical or flat disks. These are called **elliptical galaxies**. These galaxies contain very little dust and gas.

The third type of galaxy does not fit either of the past two types of galaxies.

They have no definite shape and so are termed **irregular galaxies**. These are much less common than spiral or elliptical galaxies.

Place the correct label on these galaxies.

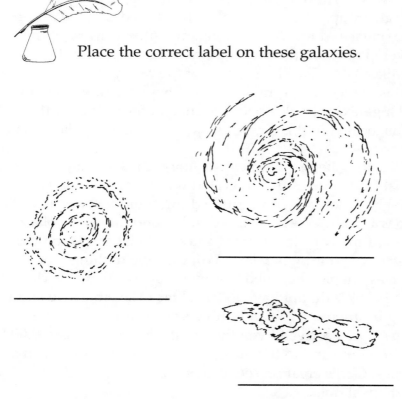

_____

_____

_____

Write the definition of galaxy in the space below.

Chapter 2 Review

1. Which star is nearest to our sun? Describe this star.

2. List three reasons why people have watched stars in the past.

3. What are two ways in which scientists categorize stars?

4. What is a constellation? Give two examples of a constellation.

5. Which two scientists guessed about the nature of galaxies? Which scientist was correct? In a paragraph, summarize his theory.

6. Define these words:
     a. multiple-star system

     b. binary star

     c. constellation

     d. composition

Chapter 3: Space Exploration
Student Objectives

My objectives are:

1. I will compare illustrations of inertia and gravity.

2. I will match the important names in space exploration with the appropriate accomplishments.

Chapter Three: Space Exploration

For centuries, human beings have dreamed of exploring the universe beyond Earth. However, that dream did not come true until October 4, 1957, when a Russian satellite, Sputnik 1, was successfully launched. That day began what was to be called The Space Age.

Many spacecraft have traveled beyond Earth's atmosphere, with and without human occupants, since that day. We have made enormous strides in learning about the vast expanses of our solar system and beyond. Astronauts have walked on the moon; they have lived in space for weeks at a time; they have linked two spacecraft far out in space. Astronauts also have piloted reusable spaceships and landed them back on Earth. Space information about the most distant planets, every year brings new advances into the uncharted frontier of the universe.

As you read these next sections, you will learn about how these space feats were accomplished.

SPACE EXPLORATION

Section 3-1: Motion and Gravity

In the seventeenth century, an English scientist named Sir Isaac Newton provided the knowledge necessary for space flight. Newton contributed the revolutionary theories of Motion and gravity.

Newton's theory is based on two factors: inertia and gravity. The law of inertia states that a moving object will not change speed or direction unless an outside force causes a change in its motion. If Earth was not affected by an outside force, we would travel in a straight line forever, passing new sights every day.

However, Newton explained that the reason Earth does not sail straight through the universe, is because some outside force must be acting on the planet. That force, he reasoned, is the sun's gravitational pull. The sun's gravity keeps the earth and other planets revolving around itself. These laws of gravitation and inertia provided the scientific basis for the development of rockets and orbital travel. Besides the sun and other stars, many planets and moons have a gravitational pull, Earth being one of them. A space flight begins when a spacecraft is launched beyond Earth's atmosphere. The main challenge of the launch is overcoming gravity. In order to overcome the earth's gravity, the rockets must move the space craft at a very high rate of speed. This speed gives the craft enough thrust, or push, to carry it beyond the effect of Earth's gravitational pull.

Once a spacecraft is beyond the earth's atmosphere, gravity is no longer a problem. But in space, everything is weightless. So astronauts must fasten everything down in their space capsule to keep it from floating away. Food must be squeezed from tubes. Also, since there is no gravity pulling on their bodies, astronauts do not get any exercise from routine movements. To stay in good physical shape, they must perform special exercises while they are weightless.

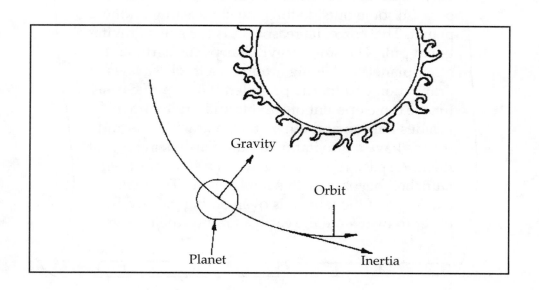

Section 3-2: Rocketry

The ideas of high-powered rocketry and space travel were not seriously considered until 1903. A Russian, Konstantin Tsiolkovsky, published a technical paper describing how rockets might reach beyond Earth's atmosphere. However, rocket technology was still in the beginning stages of development.

Then, in 1926, the first practical breakthrough occurred when Robert Goddard, an American physicist, invented a rocket that used liquid fuel. It did not fly far or for very long, but it was a great step forward.

During World War II, liquid-fuel-powered rockets were used by the Germans as weapons. After the war, Werner von Braun, director of the German rocket program, came to the United States to supervise development of its rocket program.

Other German scientists went to Russia to do similar work. Soon a race was under way between the two nations to launch artificial satellites into space.

Color the illustration below of a rocket orbiting the earth.

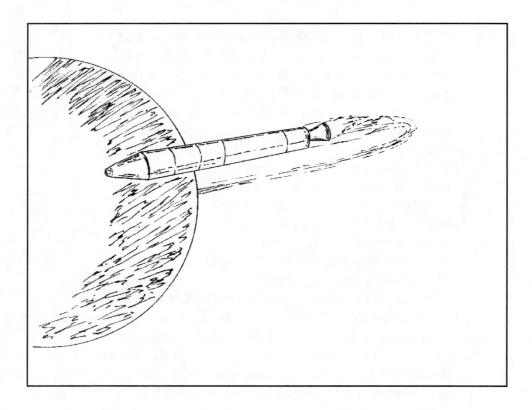

Section 3-3: Adventures in Space

Vehicles with and without crews have been launched into space. *Sputnik, Explorer, Vanguard, Luna, Pioneer, Mariner,* and others are spacecraft without a human crew. These vehicles have been put to a variety of uses. In some cases, the flights are like mechanical scouts that check out unknown territory. Only when it has been proven that it is safe for humans to go are flights with crews allowed to follow.

Surveyor 1 and *Surveyor 2* were spacecraft without crews that sent back data from the moon. This data was later used when astronauts were sent to the moon for the first time. Other unmanned satellites such as *Voyager 2*, have been sent to explore Saturn, Uranus, and Neptune. These three planets are so far from Earth that astronauts cannot, at present, travel to them and return.

Satellites carrying human crews have traveled to the moon and back. Others have orbited the earth for days, weeks, even months at a time. During these flights, astronauts test equipment, gather data on many scientific subjects, and study the effects of outer space on people.

Much can be learned from sending up pilotless spacecraft, but there is a limit to the information that can be gathered this way. For example, only by sending humans into space can we determine how space conditions affect the human body.

A number of space voyages have included space walks. A space walk is an action requiring an astronaut to work outside the craft. During this time, the astronaut wears a many-layered space suit, which protects the body from the sun's radiation and from particles of space dust called micro-meteoroids.

A space-walking astronaut is always attached to the craft by a long, flexible tube. This tube has radio transmission lines and carries oxygen from the craft to the astronaut. Not only does it keep the astronaut breathing and in communication with others, the tube is a lifeline. If it were cut, the astronaut would drift off into space.

In order to return to Earth, an orbiting spacecraft must be pointed in the right direction and must fire rockets that slow its speed. The slowing allows gravity to pull the craft back toward Earth. As the craft heads back to Earth, parachutes are released automatically. These parachutes help slow the craft even more and steady it. The craft floats down to Earth.

The main problem during the return flight of any spacecraft is the heat that builds up as it re-enters the Earth's atmosphere at high speed. This is due to the friction, or rubbing, of the craft against the air it is passing through. All spacecraft are protected against this intense heat by heat shields. The heat shield of the space shuttle, for example, is made of many ceramic titles.

Activity: View Movie

With parental permission, view the movie, Apollo 13, and note the importance of the heat shield. Before viewing, read what's next, which explains details about a trip to the moon.

On July 20, 1969, the first lunar landing took place. On that occasion, two Americans, Neil Armstrong and Edwin Aldrin, walked on the moon's surface. Their mission was followed by five more United States moon trips.

On every American lunar mission, a lunar module made a soft landing on the moon's surface. And each time, astronauts set up scientific equipment and carried out scientific experiments.

When they were finished, they launched their module from the moon and reattached it to the orbiting Apollo spacecraft. Each mission ended with a return journey to Earth.

 Match the person with the appropriate accomplishment.

a. Robert Goddard
b. Sir Isaac Newton
c. Konstantin Tsiolkovsky
d. Werner von Braun
e. Neil Armstrong and Edwin Aldrin

_____ 1. He published a technical paper describing how rockets might reach beyond Earth's atmosphere.

_____ 2. He contributed the revolutionary theories of motion and gravity that later provided knowledge necessary for space flight.

_____ 3. The director of the German rocket program during World War II who later supervised the development of the United States' rocket program.

_____ 4. The first humans to set foot on the moon.

_____ 5. An American physicist who invented a rocket that used liquid fuel.

Chapter 3 Review

1. What is the main challenge of a spaceship launch?

2. What are some activities astronauts must perform when they are weightless?

3. Name one important space expedition and describe it in a paragraph.

Learning about God's vast solar system shows us what a creative God we serve. Each planet is different and special. Learning about the other planets in our solar system also helps us to realize how special our own planet is. God designed Earth with carefulness and precision, so that life could live abundantly on it. We are God's masterpiece! Now, let's chart our course for Earth to learn in depth about God's favorite project!

Unit Two

God's Special Planet

Two

2

Student Objectives
Chapter 4: Earth's Interior

My objectives are:

1) I will color and label the various layers in a cross section of the Earth.

2) I will summarize the major characteristics of the Earth's inner layers in a diagram.

Chapter 4: Earth's Interior

In his hand are the deep places of the earth...
Psalm 95:4

Many tales have been spun that describe expeditions to the centers of worlds. In 1864, Jules Verne wrote *Journey to the Center of the Earth.* In the novel, *The Silver Chair,* C. S. Lewis wrote about Prince Rillian's journey to the center of Narnia. These writers were not the only humans to be fascinated with a world's interior. Scientists have also longed to probe the earth's center and discover its characteristics. However, the tremendous heat and pressure in the earth's interior make this region difficult to explore. In this chapter, we will explore the earth's interior!

EARTH'S INTERIOR

Section 4-1: The Earth's Mantle

We will travel deep into the earth's interior. We will push into the mantle. The mantle extends to a depth of about 2,900 kilometers below the surface. About 80 percent of the volume of the earth and about 68 percent of the planet's mass are in the mantle.

It is getting very hot, everything feels heavy, and the air in our ship feels stuffy. The density of the mantle increases with depth. The temperature and the pressure within the mantle also increase with depth. The temperature ranges from 870 degrees Celsius in the upper mantle to about 2,200 degrees Celsius in the lower mantle.

The rock in the mantle flows like a thick liquid. The high temperature and pressure in the mantle allow the rock to flow slowly, thus changing shape. When a solid has the ability to flow, it has the property of **plasticity**.

As we test a sample of the mantle, we learn that it is made mostly of the elements silicon, oxygen, iron, and magnesium.

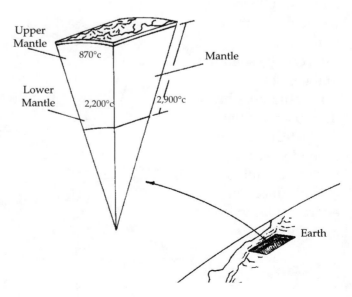

Section 4-2: The Earth's Core

We are heading straight for the center of the earth. As we leave the mantle, we notice that the liquid has changed. A test shows us that we are traveling though liquid iron and nickel. Temperature is about 2,200 degrees Celsius. This is called the **outer core,** and it is about 2,250 kilometers thick.

BUMP! We have hit something solid. As we travel up and down, we realize that the center of the earth is solid! As we travel around it, we find that the distance from the edge of the core to its center (its radius) is about 1,200 kilometers. A test of what is called the **inner core**, reveals that the earth's center is made mostly of iron and nickel. Here it is extremely hot. The temperature of the inner core reaches 5,000 degrees Celsius! If it is so hot, why isn't it melted? Iron and nickel usually melt at this temperature, but because of the enormous pressure at this depth, the particles of iron and nickel are pushed so tightly together that the elements are forced to remain solid.

Luckily our ship is not made of materials that are drawn by magnets. Otherwise, we might be stuck to the inner core forever! The solid iron in the inner core could possibly be the reason for the magnetic fields around the earth. Scientists think the iron produces an effect similar to that of a magnet.

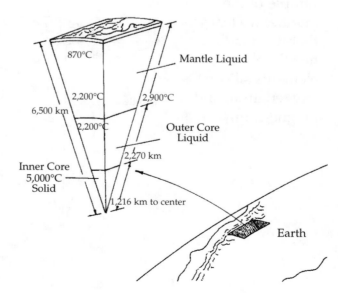

Activity: Label the cross section of the earth below using these words:

mantle
inner core
outer core

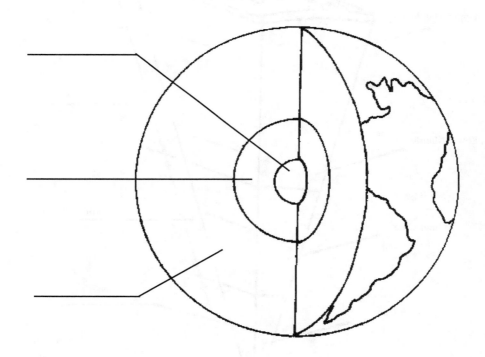

Activity: In the appropriate areas, list the elements, temperatures, and depths that make up the different layers of the earth's interior.

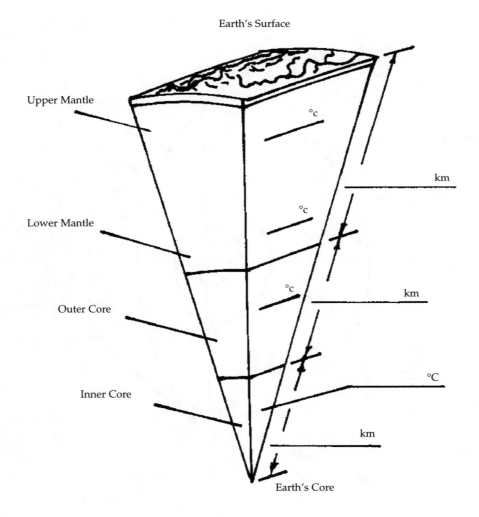

Chapter 4 Review

1. Why is the interior of the earth difficult to explore?

2. What percentages of the earth's volume and mass are located in the mantle?

3. Define plasticity.

4. Though temperatures reach 5000 degrees Celsius, the center of the Earth is solid. Explain.

5. Scientists hypothesize that the solid iron in the inner core may produce an interesting effect. What is it?

Student Objectives
Chapter 5: Earth's Crust

My objectives are:

1. I will demonstrate the relationship between the lithospheric plate and the asthenosphere in an activity.

2. I will create a play that describes the effects of an earthquake.

3. I will complete a diagram that lists the important parts of a volcano.

4. I will create a list of things that cause me stress.

Chapter 5: Earth's Crust

He puts his hand on the flint; he overturns the mountains
at the roots. He cuts out channels in the rocks,
and his eye sees every precious thing. He dams up
the streams from trickling....
                                                    Job 28:9-11

  People often use the phrase that something or someone is "as solid as a rock." They intend to describe that something or someone as being unshakable and steady. However, the phrase is rather faulty. Though the earth beneath us seems strong and steady, it actually is floating on a liquid mantle we learned about in the previous chapter. Our continents are moving. And, as anyone who has experienced an earthquake knows, our steady buildings and the land beneath them can be shaken, buckled, flattened, and folded, all in a matter of seconds.

  While it takes humans weeks, months, even years to significantly alter the earth's surface, God can change things in minutes and seconds. We have talked about being thankful for God's special designs for us. However, it is also important to reverently praise his mighty power and might. In this chapter we will learn about the surface of our earth -- the part of Earth on which we live. We will also learn the many ways that God changes the earth's surface, always remembering that it is God who is in control.

Section 5-1: Forming the Earth's Crust

The earth's crust is its thin outermost layer. It is similar to the peel on an apple. All life on Earth exists on or within a few hundred meters above the crust. Most of the crust cannot be seen because it is covered with soil, rock, and water.

We will have to travel far back in time to watch the earth's crust form. If you look down, you will see a hot liquid bubbling up. Do you know what that liquid is? It is liquid rock coming up from the depths of the earth. As it nears the surface, it begins to cool and harden. Steam is everywhere. This type of rock is called **igneous.** The word igneous means "born of fire."

Now we will travel to another place. We will not be able to see this type of rock form because it takes years and years. Think of the weight of millions of tons of small pieces of rock and sand being pressed together. As they are cemented together over long periods of time, they form what is called **sedimentary rock**.

A third type of rock, **metamorphic rock**, is formed when igneous and sedimentary rocks are changed by heat, pressure, or the action of chemicals.

How thick is the earth's crust? To answer that question, we shall travel to the lowest depths of the earth's outer layer — the ocean floor. The ocean floor is still, for the most part, unexplored territory. Even though scientists have traveled to the moon and beyond, our own ocean floor still awaits discovery. As we travel to the bottom of the ocean and measure the earth's crust, we find that it is less than 10 kilometers thick. Its average thickness is only about 8 kilometers thick. A test of oceanic crust shows that it is made mostly of silicon, oxygen, iron, and magnesium.

Now we must rise to the surface of the water, and ascend to the highest parts of a continent — its mountains. Beneath mountains, continental crust is much thicker. Under this particular mountain, the crust's thickness is greater than 70 kilometers! As we come down the mountain and measure an average part of the continent, we find that it has a thickness of about 32 kilometers. Continental crust is made mostly of silicon, oxygen, aluminum, calcium, sodium, and potassium.

This crust that we have measured at various places makes up the upper part of the **lithosphere**. The lithosphere is the solid topmost part of the earth. It is between 50 and 100 kilometers thick and is broken up into large sections called lithospheric plates. There are at least seven major plates.

The lithospheric plates move over the upper part of the mantle called the asthenosphere. When we explored the earth's interior and learned about its different layers, we learned that the mantle is a thick layer of molten rock. The asthenosphere is a thin layer of hot, molten material at the top of the mantle that flows easily.

Activity: Use a slice of bread to represent a lithospheric plate and a layer of jelly or honey spread on a piece of cardboard to represent the asthenosphere. Place the bread on top of the jelly or honey. Hold the honey and slice of bread at an incline and observe what happens.

Section 5-2: Earthquakes

People often forget about the power of nature until a catastrophe hits. An earthquake or volcanic eruption will quickly remind those it affects just how mighty nature is.

We will begin by traveling back in time to San Francisco on October 17, 1989. It is the World Series. People have filled Candlestick Park in San Francisco to watch the Giants play the Oakland Athletics. Looking from up above, we have a perfect view of the game. Before it begins, however, loud noises begin to assail our ears. We look beyond the park and see buildings collapsing. Parts of the city are twisting and folding. Fires leap up from all over the city. Gas mains explode. What was about to be an enjoyable experience has turned into a horrific, and unforgettable, nightmare.

Now let's travel to a distant ocean coast. We will watch from above because it is too dangerous to be on the ground. If you look out toward the horizon, you can see a huge wave. It is 20 meters high, about as high as a six-story building. Out there in the ocean, it is traveling toward us at speeds of 700 to 800 kilometers per hour. As it nears the coast, it slows down to about 50 kilometers pre hour. Imagine! A six-story building traveling toward us at highway speed! As it crashes on the shore, building are tackled.

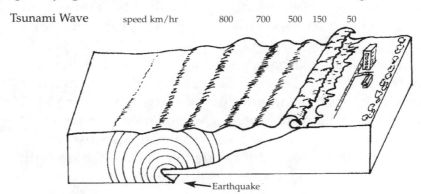

Tsunami Wave   speed km/hr   800   700   500   150   50

←—Earthquake

Though our buildings, farms, parks, and houses may seem solid and well built, we must remember that the ground beneath us, the earth's crust, is continually moving. The surface of the earth often moves in dramatic ways, such as in an **earthquake**. An earthquake is the shaking and trembling that results from the sudden movement of part of the earth's crust.

When rocks in the earth's crust break, it has the same effect as throwing a pebble in a pond. Earthquake waves travel through the earth in all directions. The ground shakes, trembles, and sometimes rises and falls like waves in an ocean. The motion of the ground causes buildings, trees, and telephone poles to sway and fall. Loud noises can sometimes be heard coming from the ground.

The most common cause of earthquakes is faulting. A **fault** is a break in the earth's crust. During faulting, parts of the earth's crust are pushed together or pulled apart. There are many faults extending over the earth's surface. The San Andreas Fault in California extends along the Pacific coast and goes directly through the city of San Francisco. It is about 960 kilometers long and 32 kilometers deep. The land to the west of the San Andreas fault is slowly moving north, and the land to the east is moving south.

Another type of earthquake begins on the ocean floor. The giant sea waves it often produces are called **tsunamis** (tsoo-NAH-meez). When a tsunami strikes the coast, it can cause great damage.

Scientists study earthquakes by studying their waves. These waves are called **seismic waves**. Scientists have learned much about earthquakes and the interior of the earth by studying seismic waves. The instrument that scientists use to detect and measure seismic waves is called a **seismograph**. Scientist who study earthquakes use the **Richter scale** to calculate the strength of an earthquake. This instrument was created by California scientists Charles Richter and Beno Gutenberg in 1935. Any number above 6 indicates a very destructive earthquake. As you might imagine, an earthquake assigned the number 10 would be truly devastating. In their study of earthquakes, scientists hope to improve their ability to accurately predict them, so people can be warned.

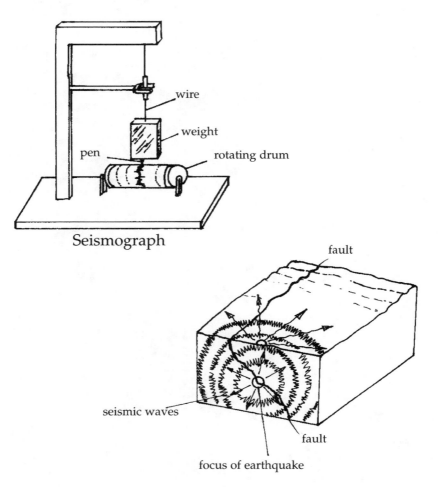

Seismograph

Activity: Create a play about a town that is devastated by an earthquake, and how the people build their lives again. After it is written, cast and direct your friends in your play and perform it in front of an audience.

Section 5-3: Volcanoes

We will have to travel back in time again. It is May, 1980. For some time, Mount. St. Helens in the state of Washington has been showing signs that it will erupt. The mountain is beautiful, symmetrical, with a perfect rounded top. Suddenly, the mountain begins to rumble, and erupts with such force that ash, rock, and lava is shot miles into the air. A bilious cloud of ash dwarfs the mountain as it rises in the air. A huge part of the side of the mountain is destroyed and races down the mountain in a giant landslide. It is a sad and awesome day.

Volcanoes are another example of how the earth's crust is in motion. Deep within the earth, under tremendous pressure and at extreme temperature, rock exists as a hot liquid called magma. This molten rock is found in pockets called magma chambers. Magma works its way toward the earth's surface through what is called a volcano. When magma reaches the surface, it is called lava. Lava is so hot that it incinerates every burnable thing in its path.

A volcano has what is called a vent. A vent is the opening from which lava erupts. Volcanoes often have more than one vent. If there is more than one vent, lava will sometimes pour from the side of a volcano as well as from the top.

There is often a funnel-shaped pit or depression at the top of a volcanic cone called a crater. If a crater becomes very large as a result of the collapse of its walls, it is called a caldera. A volcano's crater or calderas was at one time quite hot and contained bubbling lava.

Complete the illustration below. color the magma red. Color the volcano brown. Color the lava orange. Color the crater blue.

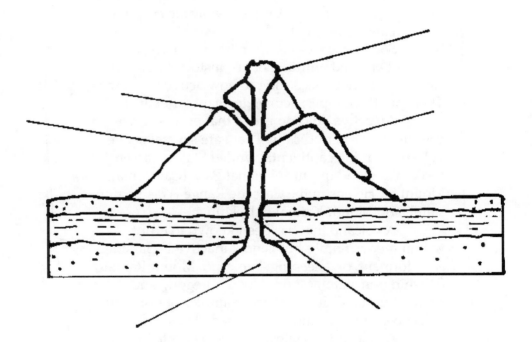

Not all volcanic eruptions are alike. Some eruptions are quiet, with lava slowly oozing from a vent. Other eruptions are very violent, with lava and other materials being hurled hundreds of miles into the air. Gases from within the earth's interior mix with huge quantities of volcanic dust and ash, and rising into the air as great dark clouds that can be seen from many kilometers away. A violent volcanic eruption is truly an awesome sight.

Some volcanoes erupt fairly regularly; others have not erupted within modern history. Scientists classify volcanoes according to how active they are. There are three types: active, dormant, or extinct.

An active volcano is one that erupts either continually or periodically. There are several active volcanoes in the continental United States: Lassen Peak in Lassen Volcanic National Park (California), Mount St. Helens in the Cascade Range (Washington state), and Mount Katmai (Alaska).

A volcano that has been known to erupt within modern times but is now inactive is classified as a dormant, or "sleeping," volcano. Mount Rainier (Washington state), Mount Hood (Oregon), and Mount Shasta (California) are examples of dormant volcanoes in the continental United States.

A volcano not known to have erupted within modern history is classified as an extinct volcano. But even so-called extinct volcanoes can prove unpredictable. Both Lassen Peak and Mount St. Helens suddenly erupted after long periods of inactivity.

Section 5-3: Stress on the Earth's Crust

The word "stress" is often used today. What are some things that cause you stress? List these things on the lines below:_____

_____

_____

_____

_____

_____

_____

_____

The earth also experiences stress. This kind of stress is different than what you experience. While you may feel pushing and pulling on your emotional self, the earth's stress is caused by the pushing and pulling on the earth's crust. The rocks that make up the earth's crust are squeezed together, melted, pulled apart, or twisted. It is as if a giant hand is always working to push, pull, and bend the crust. You know that volcanoes and earthquakes result from changes in the crust. In this chapter, you will learn about how the earth's crust is changed in other ways.

As you have just read, stress pushes and pulls on the earth's crust. As the rocks of the crust undergo stress, the movement causes the rocks to break, tilt, and fold. The breaking, tilting, and folding of rocks is called deformation.

There are three types of stress, each of which deforms the crust in a different way. The three types of stress are compression, tension, and shearing. Refer to the illustration below as you read about these types of stress.

Compression squeezes the rocks of the crust. This often causes the particles in the crustal rocks to move closer together, making the rocks denser and smaller in volume. Like a trash compactor, compression squeezes a large amount of matter into a smaller amount of space. As crustal rocks are compressed, they are pushed both higher up and deeper down. Imagine you are squeezing clay in your hand. As you squeeze the clay, some of it is pushed out of the opening at the top of your fist and some of it is pushed out of the bottom. This is how the earth's crust is raised and deepened.

Tension pulls on the rocks of the crust, causing them to stretch out over a larger area. Like a rubber band being stretched, a rock under tension becomes thinner in the middle.

Shearing pushes rocks of the crust in opposite directions. This causes the rocks to twist or tear apart. During shearing, rocks are not compressed or stretched. They simply bend or break apart.

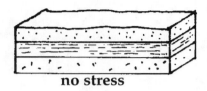

no stress

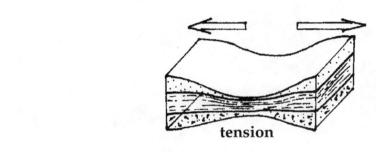

tension

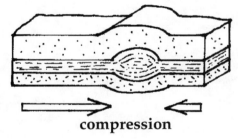

compression

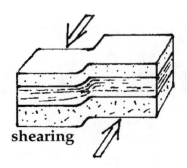

shearing

143

EARTH'S CRUST

Section 5-4: Moving the Earth's Crust

In the Bible, Jesus talks about how much faith it take to move mountains (the faith of a mustard seed). Yet, God does not just move mountains. He moves much larger pieces of the earth's crust. How does God do that? God moves the earth's crust in many ways. Two important ways in which he does this are called **faulting** and **folding**.

Stress sometimes causes rocks to break. A break or crack along which rocks move is called a **fault**. The rocks on one side of the fault slide past the rocks on the other side of the fault. Movements along a fault can be up, down, or sideways. Earthquakes often occur along faults in the earth's crust.

Sometimes when stress is applied to the rocks of the crust, the rocks bend but do not break. The rocks bend in much the same way a rug wrinkles as it is pushed across the floor. A bend in a rock is called a **fold**.

Folds vary in size. Some folds are so small that you need a magnifying glass to see them. Others are large enough to form mountains. The Appalachian Mountains in the eastern United States are a folded mountain chain that extends from Canada to Alabama.

Many factors determine whether rocks will fault or fold. One factor is temperature. The hotter the temperature, the more likely it will fold. Think of a candy bar. If you put it in the freezer, it will easily snap in two when stress is applied. The candy bar faults. However, left in a hot car for a few minutes, the candy bar will easily bend or fold.

Another factor that determines faulting or folding is pressure. If a lot of pressure is applied to the rocks, they are more likely to fold.

Rock type is another factor that will affect the process of faulting or folding. Some types of rock break easily under stress. These rocks are said to be brittle. Sandstone is a good example of this type of rock. Rock that bends easily under stress, such as rock salt, is said to be ductile. Ductile rocks are more likely to fold, and brittle rocks are more likely to fault.

How the stress is applied is another factor that determines faulting or folding. Stress that is applied suddenly will be more likely to cause faulting. Stress that is applied gradually will be more likely to result in folding.

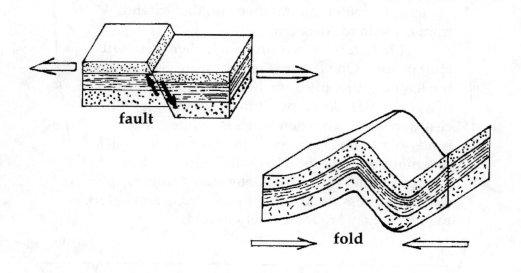

fault

fold

Section 5-5: The Floating Crust

Another process in which God moves the earth's crust is called isostasy. Perhaps you remember that beneath the earth's crust is a layer called the mantle is much denser than the crust. The solid, rocky crust floats on the mantle.

The floating crust pushes down on the mantle. The mantle pushes up on the crust. Thus, if material is added to an area of the crust, that area will float lower on the mantle. If material is removed, that area will float higher. So the crust is always balanced on the mantle. A balance exists between the downward force of the crust and the upward force of the mantle. The balancing of these two forces is called isostasy.

For example, certain low-lying regions such as Norway, Sweden, and Finland have slowly risen. Because these northern European countries were covered by tons of ice thousands of years ago, the melting of the ice removed material from the crust. As a result, the land began to float higher on the mantle.

Crustal rock can also sink. The Mississippi River has dropped millions of tons of mud and sand particles into the Gulf of Mexico. You may wonder if eventually the Gulf will be filled with sand and mud! However, because of isostasy, the addition of the materials causes the gulf to sink. The depth of the Gulf has not changed. A balance is maintained between the building up and the sinking of the Gulf floor. Isn't God clever?

Chapter 5 Review

1. List the three different types of rock that form the earth's crust and summarize their main characteristics.

2. How thick is the earth's crust?

3. Define earthquake. Then summarize how scientists study earthquakes, using these words: seismic waves, seismograph, and Richter scale.

4. What is a fault?

5. What is the relationship between magma and lava?

6. What is the difference between a crater and a caldera?

7. How do scientists classify volcanoes? List and define the three different categories.

8. How does the earth experience stress? List the three types of stress and define them.

9. Differentiate between a fault and a fold.

10. Define isostasy.

Student Objectives
Chapter 6: Earth's Landm Msses

My objectives are:

1. I will label the major continents and oceans on a map.

2. I will define and draw a picture of these words: plateau, plain, and mountain.

3. I will create a map that leads from my home to one of my favorite places.

4. Using an atlas or a globe, I will locate places that are crossed by certain meridians named in the book.

5. Using a map, I will identify the times in certain places by comparing them with given situations in the book.

6. I will label the coordinates of various ships on a map using latitude and longitude.

Chapter 6: Earth's Landm Msses

...His hands formed the dry land.
Psalm 95:5

We have viewed our planet from space and studied the earth in relationship to the other planets in our solar system. We have also explored the interior of the earth and studied the earth's crust. Now, we will look at Earth once again from a distance. To see Earth in its entirety, we will have to travel away from it, almost as if we were taking a giant step backwards to get a better view of a painting. Few people have ever seen Earth from space, yet many know what it looks like. How? As you look down at Earth, you will notice that Earth looks very similar to the many maps and illustrations that you have seen. These maps and illustrations of the earth are true to the real picture of Earth, only after a long process.

In centuries past, maps of Earth were drawn by the skilled hands of artists. Yet, because people could not see Earth from a distance, you can imagine the difficulties they had in accurately portraying the earth as it really is.

For example, before Columbus discovered the Americas, European maps would have left out these vast continents completely. As people explored planet Earth, maps became more accurate. By the middle of the eighteenth century, maps showed the Earth's land areas in the same shapes and sizes you see on maps today. Now, there is a new type of Earth map that is made from thousands of images relayed by satellites. As our maps improve, we are better able to see just how remarkably beautiful Earth is. God truly has formed our land masses with the hands of an artist. He has carefully designed a masterpiece. Let's look at the earth with new eyes--eyes that are opened to God's workmanship.

Section 6-1: The Continents

Look out the window of my cabin and notice the shapes of the land. What you see are the major **continents** and the oceans that surround them. A continent is a land mass that measures millions of square kilometers and rises a considerable distance above sea level. There are seven continents on the earth: Asia, Africa, Europe, Australia, North America, South America, and Antarctica. These continents join together to form land masses. The largest land mass on Earth is formed by the joint continents of Asia, Africa, and Europe. See the illustration below. The second largest land mass consists of the continents of North America and South America.

The third and fourth land masses are single continents: Antarctica and Australia. Antarctica is different from the other continents in many ways. It is almost completely covered by a thick icecap. In fact, the Antarctic ice cap is the largest in the world and covers an area of 34 million square kilometers! It contains 90 percent of the ice on the earth's surface, and it is the coldest place on Earth. In July 1993, the temperature in Vostok, Antarctica, dropped to -89.2 degrees Celsius, the lowest temperature ever recorded on Earth.

Antarctica has only recently been explored. In fact, the first known exploration of Antarctica occurred in 1901. Since then, many scientific stations have been built on the continent to study life, the land beneath the ice, and the conditions in the atmosphere. Today, one of the major areas of study is the depletion of the ozone layer over Antarctica. Several "holes" have been discovered, and scientists are trying to determine the possible effects. Because of the extreme cold, however, the scientists cannot live and work there permanently.

Australia is the smallest land mass still considered a continent. Sometimes Australia is referred to as the island continent. Why do you think that is so?

Correctly label the continents on the map below.

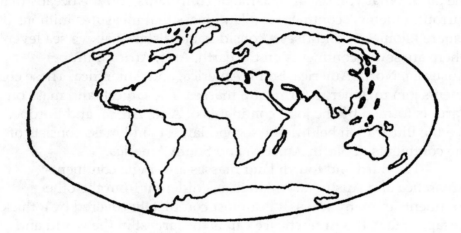

Earth's Continents

1. North America
2. South America
3. Europe
4. Africa
5. Asia
6. Australia
7. Antarctica

Section 6-2: Topography

If you run your hand over the surface of the earth, what would it feel like? Would it be smooth like ball, or fuzzy like a peach, or bumpy like a rock? The answer is that it would be like all these things and more. The earth has a varied surface that is always changing. Wind, heat, running water, earthquakes, volcanoes, and glaciers all change the surface of the earth. Humans alter the earth's surface as they flatten it for farmland, towns and cities, or build dams that slow the water flow and widen the rivers.

The shape of the earth's surface is called its **topography**. The earth's topography is made up of different kinds of **landscapes**. A landscape is a physical feature of the earth's surface found in an area. There are three types of landscape regions: mountains, plains, and plateaus. Each type has different characteristics. One characteristic of landscape regions is **elevation**, or height above sea level. Another characteristic is **relief**, or the differences in elevation within a region. A place that has very high and low places is said to have a high relief. A place that is flat, however, is said to have a low relief.

Mountains are natural land forms that reach high elevations, have narrow tops and steep sides, and have a very high relief. Mountains can be formed in several ways. Some mountains result from the folding or breaking of the earth's surface. Other mountains are created when hot magma, or liquid rock, from the earth's interior breaks through the earth's surface.

The highest mountain in the world in Mount Everest. Mount Everest is part of the Himalayas, the highest mountain range on land. Of the world's 109 peaks that are more than 7,200 meters high, 96 are located in the Himalayas. Mount Everest is 8,848 meters high. That's more than 8 kilometers! The highest mountain in the United States is Mount McKinley in the state of Alaska. It is more than 6 kilometers high! What mountains are closest to your home?

Another type of landscape region is made up of **plains**. Plains are flat land areas that do not rise far above sea level. Therefore, they have a low elevation and a low relief. The plains usually have broad rivers and streams, grasses, and good soil for farming.

Plateaus are broad, flat areas that rise more then 600 meters above sea level. Some plateaus reach elevations of more than 1,500 meters. Plateaus are not considered mountains because their surfaces are flat. Like plains, plateaus have low relief. Unlike plains, plateaus rise much higher above sea level.

Plateaus often have the same landscape for thousands of kilometers. Most are dry, nearly desert areas, and are often used for grazing cattle, sheep, and goats. Plateaus in the western United States are rich in coal and mineral deposits such as copper and lead.

Some plateaus have been deeply cut by streams and rivers that form canyons. The Colorado River cuts through the Colorado Plateau to form the Grand Canyon in Arizona. The river flows 1.5 kilometers lower than the surface of the surrounding plateau. Have you ever visited the Grand Canyon or seen pictures of it?

In the squares below, define the words and then draw a picture of the word.

plateau	plain	mountain

Section 6-3: Maps and Globes

A **map** is a drawing of the earth, or a part of the earth, on a flat surface. There are maps that show a small part of Earth's surface, such as the map of your hometown. There are also maps that show all of the earth's surface. Maps are often grouped together in a type of book that is called an atlas.

Activity

Look through an atlas and visit a place in your imagination. Write a story about your adventures.

A **globe** is a round model of the earth. It shows the shapes, sizes, and locations of all the earth's landmasses and bodies of water. A globe is the most accurate way of representing Earth.

Both maps and globes are drawn to **scale**. A scale compares distances on a map or globe to the actual distances on Earth. For example, 1 centimeter on a map might equal 10 kilometers on the earth. Different maps may have different scales, but all maps should have a scale. A scale is important because it keeps the sizes of the earth's features in proper relationship.

Draw a map below that leads from your home to one
of your favorite places. Be sure to include a scale.

Section 6-4: Meridians and Longitude

Look at a world map or globe. You may notice many straight lines on it. Some of the lines run between the North and South poles of the earth. These lines are called **meridians**. Because meridians run north and south, they measure distance east and west. The measure of distance east and west of the meridians is called **longitude**. Meridians are used to measure longitude.

The distance around the earth, or any circle, is 360 degrees. Each meridian marks 1 degree of longitude around the earth. However, not all meridians are drawn on a map or globe. Just think how crowded the map or globe would be if 360 meridians were drawn! Usually, meridians are drawn every 15 degrees, beginning with 0 degrees. The 0 degree meridian is called the **prime meridian**.

Meridians to the east of the prime meridian are called east longitudes. Meridians to the west of the prime meridian are called west longitudes. The east longitudes cover half the earth, and the west longitudes cover the other half of the earth. Because half the distance around a circle is 180 degrees, meridians of east and west longitude go from 0 degrees to 180 degrees.

Using an atlas or globe, name a place that is crossed by these meridians.

45° E _____

30° W _____

15° W _____

128° E _____

180° _____

90° W _____

Section 6-5: Time Zones

Do you have a relative or friend who lives across the United States? If so, you may know that when it is 6 p.m. at your house, it is a different time at his house. The reason for this has to do with the earth's day, or period of rotation. On Earth, a day is 24 hours long. During these 24 hours, the earth makes one complete rotation. The distance around any circle, including the earth, is 360 degrees. In one day, the earth rotates 360 degrees.

If you divide 360 degrees by the number of hours in a day (24), you will find that the earth rotates 15 degrees every hour. Thus, the earth has been divided into 24 zones of 15 degrees of longitude each. These zones are called time zones. A time zone is a strip of the earth in which all areas have the same local time.

For example, using the map at the end of this section, you will notice that it is midnight in Los Angeles, California. If you follow you finger up the time zone, you will notice that Portland, Oregon, and Seattle, Washington, are in the same time zone. It is also midnight in those places. But what about Salt Lake City, Utah? It is one time zone away from Los Angeles, California. What time is it in Nashville, Tennessee, or Boston, Massachusetts? Put your guesses below, and then read further to check you answers.

If it is midnight in Los Angeles, California, it is _____ in Salt Lake City, Utah, _____ in Nashville, Tennessee, and _____ in Boston, Massachusetts.

When you cross from one time zone to another, the local time changes by one hour. If you're traveling east, you add one hour for each time zone you cross. If you're traveling west, you subtract one hour for each time zone you cross.

Thus, if it is midnight in Los Angeles, California, it will be 1 a.m. in Salt Lake City, Utah. In Nashville, Tennessee, it will be 2 a.m., and in Boston, Massachusetts, it will be 3 a.m. Much too early in the morning!

Is it possible to make time stand still? Let's find out. We will take a 24-hour trip around the world in just a few minutes. We'll leave Miami at 1 p.m. on Sunday and go west. Are you ready? Count down! Blast off! Our launch is successful.

Because we are traveling west, we need to subtract one hour for each time zone we cross. One time zone! It is noon. Two time zones! It is 11 a.m. Seven time zones. It is 6 a.m. Eight time zones. It is 5 a.m. A few minutes more, and we will have circled the globe. We have passed 23 time zones! It is 2 p.m. And now for the landing. As we near Miami, write down the time and the day in the blanks. The local time is _____, and the day of the week is _____. We have arrived in Miami. Because you subtracted a total of 24 hours as you traveled, perhaps you think that it is still 1 p.m. on Sunday. Time hasn't moved at all, or has it?

It isn't possible to make time stand still. To avoid this confusing situation, geographers have established the **International Date Line**. The International Date Line is located along the 180th meridian. When you cross this line going east, you subtract one day. When you cross this line going west, you add one day. So in your trip around the world, you should have added one day, or gone from Sunday to Monday. You would then have arrived back in Miami, as expected, at 1 p.m. Monday afternoon.

If it were not for time zones, the sun would rise in New York City at 6 a.m., in Dallas at 7 a.m., in Denver at 8 a.m. and in Los Angeles at 9 a.m. The sun would not rise in Hawaii until 11 a.m.!

Using the map below, answer these questions. If it is such and such time in this place, what time is it in that place?

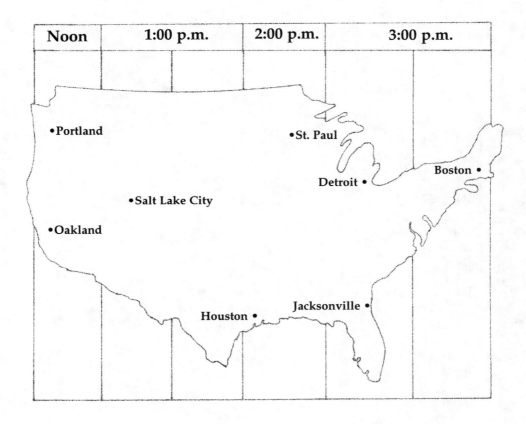

Noon	1:00 p.m.	2:00 p.m.	3:00 p.m.

•Portland

•St. Paul

Detroit •

Boston •

•Salt Lake City

•Oakland

Houston •

Jacksonville •

If it is 3p.m. in Oakland, what time is it in St. Paul?_____

If it is 2a.m. in Detroit, what time is it in Salt Lake City?_____

If it is 11:38a.m. in Boston, what time is it in Portland?_____

If it is noon in Houston, what time is it in Jacksonville? _____

169

Section 6-6: Parallels

There are also lines that run east and west across the map or globe. These lines are called **parallels**. Because parallels run east and west, they measure distance north and south. The parallel that is located half way between the North and South Poles is the **equator**. Parallels that are north of the equator are called north parallels, and parallels that are south of the equator are called south parallels.

The measure of distance north and south of the equator is called **latitude**. Parallels are used to measure latitude. The equator is labeled 0 degrees latitude. The distance from the equator to either the North or South Pole is one quarter of the distance around the earth. Recall that the distance around the earth is 360 degrees, and one quarter around the earth is 90 degrees. North and south parallels are labeled from 0 to 90 degrees. The North Pole is at 90 degrees north latitude, and the South Pole is at 90 degrees south latitude. Just as there is a meridian for every degree of longitude, there is a parallel for every degree of latitude. But not all parallels are drawn on most globes.

Activity: Charting Courses

On a globe or map, meridians and parallels form a grid of crossing lines. This grid can be used to determine the exact locations east and west of the prime meridian and north and south of the equator. Look at the map below. Ships are drawn on a map of the Pacific Ocean. Help me locate these ships by writing down the longitude and latitude of each ship.

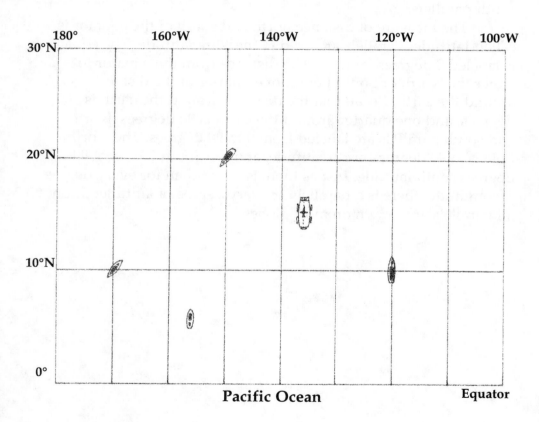

Pacific Ocean

Equator

172

Chapter 6 Review

1. Define continent.

2. Which three continents form the largest land mass on Earth?

3. Write a paragraph that describes the continent of Antarctica.

4. Define topography and landscape.

5. What is the difference between a map and a globe? Which one more accurately represents Earth?

6. Define meridian and longitude.

7. What name is given to the 0 degree meridian?

8. In a paragraph, explain the International Date Line.

9. Define parallels and latitude.

10. Which parallel is located halfway between the North and South Poles?

Student Objectives
Chapter 7: Earth's Waters

My objectives are:

1. I will list reasons why water is important.

2. I will keep a record of my water use.

3. I will create a collage that demonstrates why I appreciate water.

4. I will define "cycle" and "water cycle."

5. I will recreate the water cycle in an experiment.

6. I will create a story about the journey of a water droplet.

7. I will complete diagrams that show how ground water is stored, the major parts of a wave, the temperature zones in the ocean, and the ocean life zones in the ocean.

8. I will visit a site where there is running water and standing water.

9. I will complete a map of the three major oceans.

10. I will complete a circle graph of the ocean's elements.

11. I will draw an example of a nekton and write a caption for it.

12. I will create a model of the ocean floor.

Chapter 7: Earth's Water

"You visit the earth and water it, You greatly enrich it...
provide their grain... You water the ridges...
You settle its furrows... make it soft with showers..."
Psalms 65:9-13

We have learned about the earth's composition, surface, and land masses. However, did you know that 75 percent of the earth is covered by water? In this chapter we will learn about the waters on Earth.

Why is water important? Write your answer on the lines below.

_____

_____

_____

_____.

Water is a matter of life or death. With predators quietly waiting, many animals risk death while trying to reach water. Why? Without water, death is certain. Humans, of course, need water to survive. A person can go without food for weeks, but without water, that same person would die within a few days.

Water, however, is not only important because we need it to survive. Think of other uses for water. Activities such as washing, cooking, swimming, or fishing are a few ways we use water. Try to imagine what life would be like if we could only use water for drinking. How would we keep clean? Wash dishes? What would cool our cars? What forms of recreation would take place during the summer? It is easy to see that water is not only important to us for survival, but also for our daily lifestyles, our recreation, and its beauty. Water is a good thing — something we need, something we use, and something we enjoy. It is a gift from God!

In James 1:17, it says, "Every good gift and every perfect gift is from above and comes down from the Father of lights..." It is important to thank God for water, which is so important to us. He cares so much for us that He provides for all our needs and many of our wants.

Activity: Record of Water Use

Keep a record of how often and how many ways you use water. Starting now, write down every time you use water and the way you use it until the same time tomorrow.

Water Use Chart

Date	Use of Water

How is water important to you?

_____

_____

_____

_____

Take time to thank God for water and for all the ways we are able to use it.

Activity: How does God use water in my region?

1. Visit a lake, river, or pond near where you live. Try to see ways that water is used by other living things. Do the plants and animals in your area require much water?

2. Observe the land around you. Does it require much water? Feel the earth with your fingers. Is it dry or wet? Is it hard or soft? Try to think of reasons why it feels the way it does.

3. Because all living things require water to survive, water places are often the center of wildlife activity. Listen to all the sounds around you. Sit quietly and concentrate on how God uses water to take care of all the living things around you.

 **Activity: Thanking God for Water**

1. With a partner, write down 50 words that are related to water. (Hint: Write 10 words that are related to water and then find each one in a thesaurus. Copy the related words and then repeat the process.)

2. Using the words in your list, create 10 sentences that tell God why you appreciate water.

3. Write your five favorite sentences in any order you wish in your nicest writing or on the computer. (Suggestion: You may also cut the words or letters out of old magazines and newspapers.)

4. Decorate the borders of the page with drawings, graphics, or cut-out pictures related to water.

What is the Water Cycle?

"Do you not fear Me?" says the Lord. "Will you not tremble at My presence, who have placed the sand as the bound of the sea, by a perpetual decree, that it cannot pass beyond it? And though its waves toss to and fro, yet they cannot prevail; though they roar, yet that cannot pass over it." Jeremiah 5:22

Our earth is covered in water. Photographs of the earth from space show what astronauts call a swirling "blue planet." However, though the world is covered in water, the majority of it is *salt water*. Many living things cannot live on salt water. The salt must be taken out of it before it can be used. About 97% of Earth's water is salt water. Only 3% is fresh, and most of that is frozen in glaciers and ice caps at the North and South Poles. Only a very small percentage of fresh water is available for living things to use, which brings up a very good question. Why don't we run out of water?

In Jeremiah 5:22, it says that God placed a boundary around the oceans. Yet, if the rivers continually run into oceans, what keeps them from rising? God has created the waters so that there is a constant flow into and out of the oceans. The Bible is speaking about the water cycle in this verse. God has created this wonderful cycle so that the water supply is in balance. Though much of the earth's water is salt water, God is constantly making fresh water for living things to use. In the next chapters, we'll learn how He does that.

The word "cycle" has a variety of definitions. However, the dictionary definition that describes the meaning used in water cycle is "a periodically repeated sequence of events." Dictionary definitions are sometimes just as difficult to understand as the words they define.

Can you write a definition of cycle that is easier to understand?
Write it after the word below:

cycle: _____

_____

_____

_____

Using your definition above, give your own new definition of
"water cycle" and write it on the lines below.

water cycle: _____

_____

_____

_____

_____

_____

_____

Section 7-1: The Water Cycle

We have learned that God has created a balance in the water supply. Yet how does He do it? Let's take a journey to explore the different phases of the water cycle. We will begin by visiting the middle of one of our vast oceans. Look around. As far as your eye can see, there is water. Yet, for many living organisms, this salty, briny water cannot be used to keep them alive. They need the salts taken out of the water. They need pure, fresh water.

The first step of the water cycle needs to take place. The sun is beating down on us and as the sun heats the surface of the ocean, **evaporation** occurs. Evaporation causes the water to change from the liquid phase to the gas phase. Water — pure, fresh water — is lifted into the air. The salts remain in the ocean.

A fresh breeze kicks up and blows our hair around our faces. This same wind will carry the water vapor across the vast sea and to land. We will follow where the wind leads us. With the wind behind us, we travel across the ocean and see the shore ahead of us. As we continue over the land, water vapor continues to form. How does this happen? Water also evaporates from the land and from living things on land. This process is called transpiration.

A range of mountains rises into our view. The air has cooled. As the warm air close to the earth's surface rises, it cools. Cool air cannot hold as much water vapor as warm air. We are surrounded by fog and swirling mists. Clouds are forming. What we are experiencing is called **condensation**. Condensation is the process by which water vapor changes back to a liquid. In the cooler air, most of the water vapor condenses into droplets of water that form clouds.

The clouds continue to form, becoming heavier and more numerous. We will drop down to the land below us so we can experience this next phase in the water cycle. As our ship touches the earth's crust, we first hear a pit-pat and a drip-drop, and then we feel the drops of water landing on our heads. It is raining. The process by which water falls to the earth is called **precipitation**.

Precipitation can come in the form of rain, snow, sleet, or hail. This water is fresh water; water that helps living organisms, like ourselves, to survive.

The water cycle does not stop here. The drops of water that fall to the earth begin to trickle down ravines and valleys, both small and large. As they seek out the lower places, they gather and grow into brooks, streams, and rivers. As we follow a trickle, it merges with a stream, which joins with a river, which runs across the land and back into the ocean. We have arrived at the starting point of our journey!

The **water cycle** can be defined as the movement of water from the oceans and freshwater sources to the air and land, and finally back to the oceans again. It is a continuous chain of events. God has designed this wonderful system to give the life-sustaining liquid, water, to all of us!

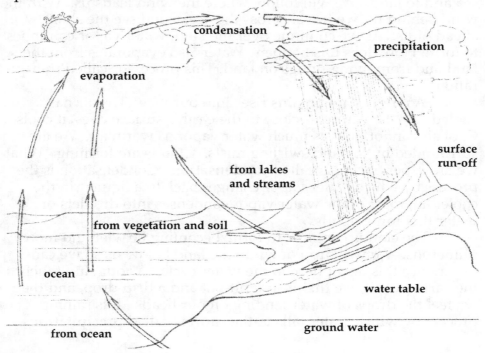

Recreating the Water Cycle

Materials: bowl, salt, wide-mouthed jar, paper cup, sand, plastic wrap, rubber band, small rock or weight.

1. Measure 1 cm from the bottom of the wide-mouthed jar and mark it.

2. Fill a bowl with water and stir in salt until no more salt will dissolve.

3. Pour the salt water to the 1 cm mark in the large jar.

4. Fill the paper cup hal full with sand and place it in the center of the wide-mouthed jar.

5. Cover the wide-mouthed jar of plastic and seal its sides with a rubber band.

6. Place a small rock or weight on the plastic wrap directly over the paper cup.

7. Place the jar in direct sunlight and wait several hours.

8. Carefully remove the plastic wrap and try to collect a few drops of water that cling to it.

9. Taste the collected water.

10. Record your observations and answer the questions on the next page.

A. What did the water taste like?

B. What is the purpose of sealing the jar?

C. What processes of the water cycle are exemplified in this model?

Journey of a Water Droplet

Imagine that you are a water droplet on a journey. Where would you begin? Which places would you go? Where would your journey end? Write a story about your adventures, using "I".

Section 7-2: Fresh Water

As we discussed before, fresh water makes up only about three percent of the earth's water. However, most of this fresh water cannot be used because it is frozen, mainly in the icecaps near the North and South Poles and in glaciers.

Frozen Water: About 85 percent of Earth's fresh water is frozen. Let's travel to a place where we can see many examples of this frozen water. We have arrived in a place covered in snow. It is snowing heavily. As the new snow falls on top of the old, the pressure causes some of the snow to change into ice. When the layers of ice become very thick and heavy, the ice begins to move. What we are seeing is the finishing touches made to a glacier. A glacier is a huge mass of moving ice and snow that forms over a long period of time. Glaciers form in very cold areas, such as high in mountains and near the North and South Poles.

Now we will travel to a high mountain. As we look down one of the deep valleys, we see that it is filled with ice. All over the surface of this sheet of ice are deep cracks called crevasses. **Valley glaciers** are long, narrow glaciers that move down the mountain valleys.

We will visit the polar regions next. Here, snow and ice have built up to form thick sheets of ice that are different from the narrow, valley glacier. As we turn to view this snowy panorama, we see that this glacier extends millions of square kilometers and is several thousand meters thick. It is called a **continental glacier**. These massive glaciers move slowly in all directions. Continental glaciers are found in Greenland and Antarctica.

We move over this vast land of ice to its edge. As we near the sea, we slowly approach the edge of a cliff.

Large chunks of ice that break off of these cliffs and drift into the sea are called **icebergs.**

As we look around us, we hear the long, mournful cry of a ship's horn and see a light in the darkness. The light is coming straight for us, slowly, steadily. We must warn the captain! We must get his attention! Let's flash every light we have! Hurry! The ship changes its direction, but barely misses us. The side of the ship scrapes against the iceberg as it passes, but there is no permanent damage. Whew! That was close!

Icebergs can pose a major hazard to ships. Icebergs are difficult to avoid because only a small part rises above the water's surface. In 1912, the ocean liner Titanic smashed into an iceberg in the North Atlantic Ocean. Many believed the ship to be unsinkable. Yet, on her maiden voyage, the ship was sunk and many lives were lost. Today, ships and planes patrol sea lanes as they look for icebergs.

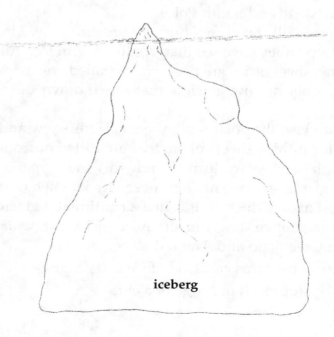

iceberg

Running Water: Most of us have visited a river or a stream. However, perhaps you have not pondered just how important rivers and streams are to our well-being. Cities and towns are built near rivers and streams where the water is used to irrigate crops, generate electricity, and drink. It is also used for household purposes and recreational purposes such as fishing, swimming, and boating.

How do these rivers and streams begin? We learned part of the answer when we journeyed through the water cycle. We watched the precipitation fall to the ground and trickle into streams and rivers. Water that enters a river or stream after a heavy rain or during a spring thaw is called **surface run-off**.

Not all of the water from precipitation that falls to the ground or from frozen water that melts goes into streams and rivers. Some of it is soaked into the soil or absorbed by the roots of the plants in the area.

Standing Water: Some of the surface run-off gets caught in low places. These standing bodies of water are called lakes or ponds. Like rivers and streams, lakes and ponds receive their water from the land. Lakes are usually large, deep depressions in the earth's crust that have filled with fresh water. Ponds are shallow depressions in the earth's crust that have filled with fresh water. They are usually smaller and not as deep as lakes.

Sometimes artificial lakes are created by damming a stream or river that runs through a low-lying area. This is called a reservoir. Reservoirs are the most frequently used sources of fresh water.

Ground Water: Some of you may not get your water from a river, lak,e or reservoir. Perhaps your water is pumped from a well. Water that is stored in the ground is called **ground water**. As you learned in the previous section, not all water trickles into streams and rivers. Some of it is soaked into the soil. Once precipitation hits the ground, it often continues to travel slowly downward through pores, or spaces, in the rocks and soil, until it reaches a layer of the earth where water cannot pass any further.

As the water seeps down, it passes through materials through which water can move quickly. These types of materials are described as **permeable**. Eventually, the water will reach an **impermeable** layer of rock. The water can pass no further. The ground water begins to fill up all the layers above it. This region that is filled with water is called the **zone of saturation**. Above the water-filled area, the ground is not as wet. This drier region where the spaces are filled mostly with air is called the **zone of aeration**. The boundary between the two zones is called the **water table**.

Enrichment Activity: Create a diagram of how ground water is stored, using the bold-faced words in this section.

Outdoor Excursion

Begin an outdoor journal. Remember to record the different animals, plants, and land forms that you see. It's also important to record any thoughts, prayers or reflections you have. Be sure to date your entries!

1. Visit a river, stream, or creek.

2. Consider this idea from an ancient philosopher: *You cannot put your foot in the same river twice.*

3. Pick out a spot and watch the water run over it. Think about how much water passes over this particular spot. How long has water been running over it? How long will water continue running over it?

4. Imagine yourself journeying to the river's source. Would it be a spring? A glacier?

5. Thank God for the beautiful balance He has created. As water leaves us, more water comes to us. God has provided for our essential needs in a very interesting way.

Section 7-3: Oceans

As we travel around the earth, you will notice that Earth's different oceans are not really separate at all. Although each ocean and sea has a separate name, all of the oceans and seas are actually one continuous body of water.

The Atlantic, Indian, and Pacific oceans are the three major oceans. Smaller bodies of water such as the Arctic Ocean, the Mediterranean Sea, and the Black Sea are considered part of the Atlantic Ocean. A sea is a part of an ocean that is nearly surrounded by land. Can you name any other seas?

The Pacific Ocean is the largest ocean on Earth. Its area and volume are greater than those of the Atlantic and Indian Oceans combined. The Pacific Ocean is also the deepest ocean. The Atlantic Ocean is the second largest ocean. Although the Indian Ocean is much smaller than the Atlantic, its average depth is greater.

Let's learn more about oceans!

Activity: Correctly label the major oceans on the map below, using a map or a globe.

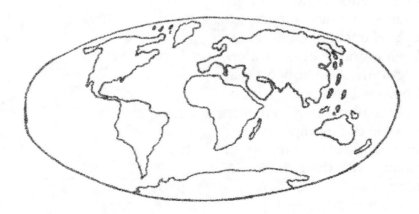

Composition of Ocean Waters

We have pulled up a bucket of ocean water and tested it to see what it contains. What elements do you think are present? Write your guesses on the line below.

_____ .

Nice work. Our tests reveal that ocean water is a mixture of gases and solids dissolved in pure water. Scientists who study the ocean, or oceanographers, have found that ocean water is about 96 percent pure water. Thus, the most abundant elements in ocean water are hydrogen (H) and oxygen (O).

The other 4 percent consists of dissolved elements. Sodium chloride is the most abundant of these dissolved elements. You may know this combination as common table salt. However, sodium chloride is only one of many salts dissolved in ocean water. Combinations of magnesium, sulfur, calcium, potassium, bromine, carbon, strontium, silicon, fluorine, aluminum, phosphorus, and iodine are also present in ocean water.

Oceanographers believe that ocean water contains all of the natural elements found on Earth. 90 elements are known to exist in nature. So far, about 85 of these have been found in ocean water. Oceanographers are hopeful that with improved technology, they will find the remaining elements.

In the circle graph, write the elements that make up ocean water along with their percentages.

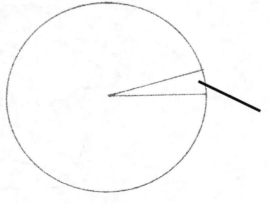

10. Name three different types of

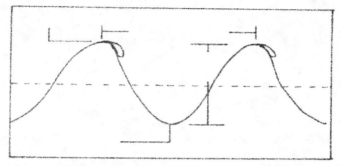

We can easily see ocean motions in the form of waves. Yet, another ocean motion is not so easily noticed with the naked eye. Below the surface, the ocean moves in the form of currents. These currents are streams in the ocean that can extend for thousands of kilometers.

There are two types of currents: **surface currents** and **deep currents**. Surface currents are caused mainly by wind patterns. They usually have a depth of several hundred meters. Surface currents that travel thousands of kilometers are called long-distance surface currents; surface currents that move over short distances are called short-distance currents. A warm current begins in a warm area, and a cold current begins in a cold area. The diagram below shows the major warm and cold surface currents of the world.

Notice in the diagram to the right that the water in the Northern Hemisphere moves in a clockwise (the same way the hands of a clock move) motion. In the Southern Hemisphere, the currents move in the opposite direction, or counterclockwise. These currents are being pushed by winds. What can you conclude about the wind patterns in each hemisphere? Winds move in a _____ motion in the Northern Hemisphere and in a _____ motion in the Southern Hemisphere.

Deep currents are caused by the differences in the density of water deep in the ocean. Think of density as the heaviness of water. Cold water is more dense than warm water. Most deep currents flow in the opposite direction from surface currents. For example, dense, cold Antarctic water sinks to the ocean floor and flows north through the world's oceans. At the same time, warm surface currents near the equator flow south toward Antarctica. As the cold water nears land, it is forced upwards, causing the deep cold currents to rise to the ocean surface. This is called an upwelling. Upwellings lift up rich food that has drifted down to the ocean floor, and attract all kinds of ocean life. Important fishing industries are built around these upwellings.

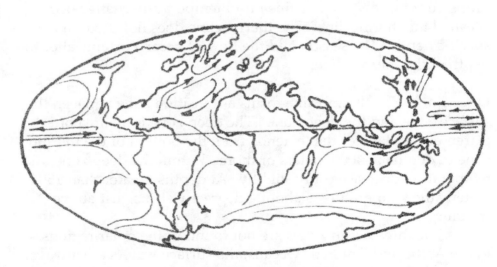

**Ocean Currents of
the World**

Temperature Zones: There are three different temperature zones in the oceans: the **surface zone, thermocline**, and **deep zone**. Let's learn about these areas of the ocean!

Surface Zone: The sun is the major source of heat for the ocean. Therefore, because the sun's energy enters the ocean at the surface, the surface zone is the warmest of all the zones. The surface zone can extend to a depth of 100-400 meters. The temperature of the water within a surface zone does not change much with depth. However, temperatures in surface zones do vary according to location and season. Water near the equator is warmer than water in regions farther north and south. Summer water temperatures are warmer than winter water temperatures.

Thermocline: Below the surface zone the temperature of the water drops very rapidly. Where this rapid temperature change occurs is called the thermocline. The thermocline does not occur at a specific depth. The season and the flow of ocean currents alter the depth of the thermocline.

Deep Zone: The thermocline forms a transition zone between the surface zone and the deep zone. The deep zone is an area of extremely cold water that extends from the bottom of the thermocline to depths of 4000 meters or more. Within the deep zone, the temperature decreases only slightly. At depths greater than 1500 meters, the temperature is about 4 degrees Celsius, just above freezing.
    The three ocean zones are not found in the polar regions. In the Arctic and Antarctic Oceans, the surface waters are always very cold. The temperature changes only slightly as the depth increases.

Label the different temperature zones in the following diagram.

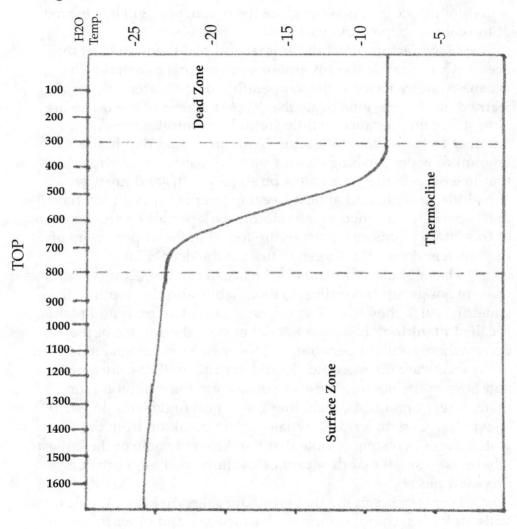

Ocean Life Forms

There is an incredible diversity of plant and animal life found in the ocean. As we explore the ocean, you will be amazed at the colors, shapes, and variety that you see.

Many factors affect the animal and plant life found in the ocean. One factor is the amount of sunlight that penetrates the ocean. Another factor is the temperature of the water. As we learned on the previous page, the deepest waters of the ocean are almost freezing because so little sunlight penetrates there. Another factor is water pressure. With increasing depth, the amount of water pushing down from above increases. Organisms that live deep in the ocean must be able to withstand great pressure, little sunlight and almost freezing temperatures. They have to be specially designed to inhabit this dark part of Earth. Because of this, more plants and animals are found in the upper layers of the ocean and near the shoreline than in the deeper layers.

The animals and plants in the ocean can be classified into three major groups according to their habits and the depth of the water in which they live. The largest group of animals and plants is called **plankton**. Plankton float at or near the surface of the ocean where sunlight penetrates. Most plankton are very small — many forms are microscopic. Plankton drifts with the currents and tides of the ocean. These organisms are the main food for many larger organisms, including the largest organisms on Earth — whales. Certain kinds of whales strain plankton from the water. It is interesting to note that the throat of some of the largest whales is so small that they cannot swallow food larger than a fifty-cent piece!

Forms of ocean life that swim are called **nekton**. Whales, seals, dolphins, squid, octopuses, barracudas, and other fishes are all nekton. Among the most feared nekton are the sharks. Some types of sharks are feared **predators** in the ocean. Predators are organisms that eat other organisms. The organisms that get eaten are called **prey**. Other nekton are shark's prey.

Organisms that live on the ocean floor are called **benthos**. Some benthos are plants that grow on the ocean floor in shallow waters. Other benthos are animals such as barnacles, oysters, crabs, and starfish. A few kinds of animal benthos live on the ocean floor in the deepest parts of the ocean. Plants are able to survive in water only where sunlight penetrates.

Activity: Draw an example of a nekton and write a caption that tells the reader something interesting about it.

Ocean Life Zones

Now, let's begin a journey through the various life zones of the ocean. As we set out from shore, you will notice that there are shallow beach areas that dry out twice a day and then become wet again. The region that lies between the low and high tide lines is called the **intertidal zone**. This region is the most changeable zone in the ocean. Sometimes it is ocean. Sometimes it is dry land. It is difficult for living things to survive in the intertidal zone. Because the tide rises and falls, organisms must be able to live without water some of the time. Organisms that live in the intertidal zone include starfish, giant limpets, clams, barnacles and sea anemones. Many of these organisms attach themselves to sand and rocks to keep from being washed out to sea. Certain worms and some kinds of shellfish burrow into the wet sand for protection.

We continue out to sea. Beneath us, the ocean shoreline gradually slopes downward. The continent we are leaving extends out under the ocean. This is called the **continental shelf**. At the end of the shelf is the **continental slope**. This marks the end of the continent, and the beginning of the ocean floor. The continental slope is steeper than the continental shelf. Beyond the continental slope lies the ocean basin with all of its interesting features that we will eventually explore.

As we continue out to sea, we begin to encounter all kinds of fishing boats. Most of the world's great fishing areas are within what is called the **neritic zone**. Fish, clams, snails, some types of whales, and lobsters are but a few of the kinds of organisms that live here. In fact, the neritic zone is richer in life than any other ocean zone. The neritic zone extends from the low-tide line to waters that have about 200 meters of depth. It ends where there is too little sunlight for seaweed to grow.

We have left the neritic zone and now are entering the **open sea zone**. As you look out over the waters, you see a massive animal, larger than our ship, surface and then sink below the waters. It is a blue whale, the largest animal on Earth. It is approximately 30 meters long! A group of dolphins, curious to see who we are, approaches the ship diving and jumping in excitement.

If all of the water beneath us was suddenly swallowed, we would be left suspended in the air 6000 meters! The open-sea zone is where the waters extend to a great depth. There are two open-ocean zones. Let's close up our ship and dive to the ocean's depths!

The first open-sea zone we will encounter is the **bathyal zone**. It begins at a continual slope and extends down about 2000 meters. Sunlight is not able to penetrate to the bottom of this zone, and thus plants are unable to grow. Look out the window. A giant squid with all of its arms trailing behind it passes by. A gulper eel wiggles its body through the dark waters. Then there is a pause, and a school of fish rapidly darts away. A minute later, we see a blue shark swim by carefully, hardly disrupting the water.

As we dive beyond 2000 meters, the **abyssal zone** begins. This is the second open-ocean zone. The abyssal zone extends to an average depth of 6000 meters. This zone has a few strange creatures that eke out an existence on these large, flat plains. No sunlight is able to penetrate to this zone. Little food is available. The water pressure is very great. The temperature is almost freezing. It is a harsh and lonely world.

Most of the animals that live here are small. Outside the window is an anoplogaster. With its needle-like teeth bared, the tiny 15-centimeter fish patrols the ocean depths in search of prey. The devilfish, 3.8 centimeters, and the anglerfish, 12.5 centimeters, are two other deep-sea dwellers. Some of the animals that live in this zone are able to make their own light.

Activity: Using the words listed below, create a crossword puzzle. The project should include a blank crossword puzzle, an answer key, a page with the ACROSS definitions, and a page with the DOWN definitions.

1. plankton

2. nekton

3. predators

4. prey

5. benthos

6. intertidal zone

7. neritic zone

8. open sea zone

9. bathyal zone

10. abyssal zone

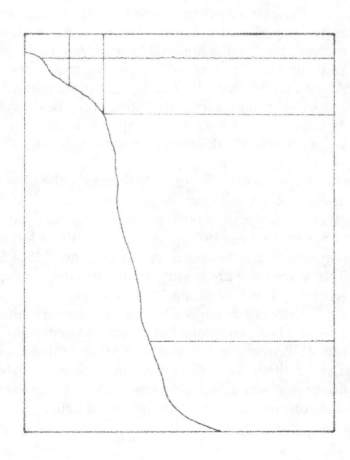

Exploring the Ocean Floor

Now that we have reached the bottom of the ocean, let's explore this interesting place. The oceans have been called the last great unexplored places on Earth. In fact, we probably know more about some of our neighbors in outer space than we do about the watery depths of our own planet. Very few scientists have ever explored the ocean floor as we are going to do now. Mapping the ocean floor is usually done by sending energy waves to the bottom of the ocean where they are reflected back to the surface and recorded.

How do you picture the ocean floor? Is it hilly or flat? Are there canyons? Does it look like the continents? Write what you think on the lines below.

_____
_____
_____
_____
_____
_____
_____.

Good work! A map of the ocean floor would look much different than a map of the continents. The ocean floor has higher mountains, deeper canyons, and larger, flatter plains than the continents. The ocean floor also has more volcanoes, and earthquakes occur with greater frequency under the ocean than on the land.

Look out the ship windows. Every direction you look, you see nothing but large, flat, empty spaces. These large flat areas on the ocean floor are called **abyssal plains**. The abyssal plains are larger in the Atlantic and Indian Oceans than in the Pacific Ocean. A test sample of the abyssal plain reveals that it is made of several layers of mud, sand, and silt. Where ocean life is not abundant, the floor of the ocean is covered with a sediment called red clay. Red clay is made of sediments carried to the oceans by rivers.

As we continue on our way, we see that straight ahead of us is a large, underwater mountain. We will slowly rise up to measure the height of this mountain. It is over 1000 meters high. Its steep sides lead to a narrow summit (or top). We also find that this mountain is volcanic. Volcanic mountains that rise more than 1000 meters above the surrounding ocean floor are called **seamounts**. Oceanographers have located more than 1000 seamounts, and they expect to find thousands more in the future. Many more seamounts have been found in the Pacific Ocean than in either the Atlantic of the Indian Ocean.

Some seamounts reach above the surface of the ocean to form islands. Perhaps the most dramatic and familiar volcanic islands are the Hawaiian Islands in the Pacific Ocean.

The island of Hawaii is the top of a great volcano that rises more than 9600 meters from the ocean floor. It is the highest mountain on Earth when measured from its base on the ocean floor to its peak.

Ahead of us is another seamount. We will pass over its top. Instead of a normal peak, this seamount has a flat top. Waves broke apart the top of this seamount that was once at sea level. This flattened volcanic seamount was then submerged and is called a **guyot**.

As we travel ahead, we see before us an unusually large mountain range. Rather than propel ourselves over it, we decide to follow along beside it. Hours and hours pass. What we find is that it appears to continue without end.

Mid-ocean ridges are some of the largest mountain ranges on Earth. These under-water mountain chains extend from the Arctic Ocean, down through the middle of the Atlantic Ocean, around Africa into the Indian Ocean, and then across the Pacific Ocean to North America in an almost continuous belt.

Mid-ocean ridges differ from continental mountain ranges in how they were formed. Continental mountain ranges were formed by the Earth's crust folding and being squeezed together. Mid-ocean ridges are formed by hot liquid rising from deep within the earth. At the surface, the molten material cools and piles up to form new crust.

Great earthquake and volcanic activity occurs in the deep crevices in and around mid-ocean ridges called rift valleys. Rift valleys are about 25 to 50 kilometers wide and 1 to 2 kilometers deep.

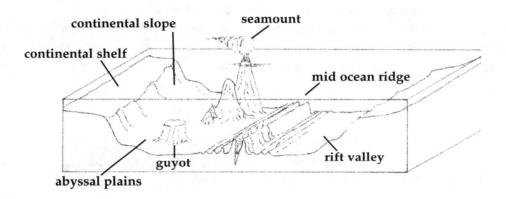

We have crossed an abyssal plain, passed by a group of seamounts and an underwater mountain range, and now we have reached the edges of the Pacific Ocean floor. Below us is a long, narrow crevice called the Mariana Trench. We maneuver over to a spot in the Mariana Trench called Challenger Deep. We dive into it to explore its depths. We drop 5000 meters, 8000 meters, 10,000 meters, then 11,000 meters! This is the deepest spot known on Earth. People often visit the Empire State Building in New York because of its great height (430 meters). To reach the ocean surface from the bottom of Challenger Deep would take 26 Empire State Buildings stacked on one another.

The deepest parts of the ocean are not in the middle of the ocean floor. The greatest depths are found in trenches along the edges of the ocean floor. Trenches are long, narrow cracks in the earth that can be more than 11,000 meters deep.

As we near the surface of the ocean and approach a tropical island, we notice large masses and ridges of limestone rocks. This is a colorful creation. We see beautiful, exotic, and strange organisms living within and swimming about the structure.

215

We find that these limestone structures contain shells of animals. What we are looking at is called a coral reef.

The organisms that build reefs can survive only in warm waters and where sunlight can penetrate. Thus, coral reefs are found only in tropical waters and near the surface.

Activity

Create a model of the ocean floor using plaster of Paris, clay, or paper-mache. Show all the features of the ocean floor and label them. Show your friends your creation!

As you can see, the ocean is a very interesting place to explore. It is also very important to our lives and well-being. The ocean provides food, fresh water, salt, and other important resources. God has given us a rich gift in the ocean.

Chapter 7 Review

1. Why is water important?

2. Name five ways that humans use water.

3. Why should we thank God for water? (Hint: Read James 1:17.)

4. What percentage of the earth is covered by water?

5. What percentage of the earth's water is saltwater? What percentage is fresh?

6. Explain in a paragraph why we never run out of fresh water.

7. List the major phases in the water cycle and define them.

8. Compare a valley glacier with a continental glacier.

9. Define iceberg.

10. Name three different types of standing water.

11. What are the three main oceans of the world?

12. What is a sea?

13. Scientists who study the ocean are called _____.

14. Compare surface currents with deep currents.

15. Match these words with the correct definition.

abyssal plains   coral reef   trench   rift valley
seamount   guyot   mid-ocean ridge

_____ 1. Long, narrow cracks that form the deepest part of the
ocean; found along the edges of the ocean floor; can be more than
11,000 meters deep.

_____ 2. Volcanic mountains that rise more than 1000 meters
above the surrounding ocean floor.

_____ 3. Limestone structures found in tropical waters that contain the shells of animals.

_____ 4. Underwater mountain chains that are formed by hot liquid rising from deep within the earth.

_____ 5. Deep crevices in and around mid-ocean ridges where
earthquake and volcanic activity occur.

_____ 6. A seamount that was once at sea level, but waves have
broken apart the top and submerged it.

_____ 7. Large, flat areas on the ocean floor.

Student Objectives
Chapter 8: Earth's Atmosphere

1. I will color and label a circle graph that shows the percentage of gases in the earth's atmosphere.

2. I will complete a diagram that shows the different layers of the atmosphere.

3. I will compare the weather forecast with the actual weather for several days and record my findings on a chart.

4. I will label diagrams that represent a land breeze and a sea breeze.

5. I will illustrate three different types of clouds and three different types of precipitation and define these words.

6. I will list the types of weather I like and dislike.

7. I will create a rain gauge in an experiment.

8. I will make educated guesses about the types of storms that are described in the book and correct my answers.

9. I will complete an illustration of the different types of climates.

Chapter 8: Earth's Atmosphere

We have studied Earth from space. We have also learned about Earth's interior, crust, land masses, and waters. Now it is time to travel through the atmosphere. The atmosphere is a mixture of gases that surround the earth. The atmosphere acts as a protective bubble for all living things. God has carefully created the atmosphere to protect us from the dangers of space and to provide us with essential gases to survive.

After learning about the atmosphere in general, we will focus on weather. Perhaps you have watched the weather forecast. Today, many people watch this part of the news to find out whether tomorrow will be a good day for a picnic. However, wrong weather forecasting has much more serious consequences for some people than missing a picnic. Farmers must watch the weather to know when to plant and harvest. Fisherman watch the weather to avoid storms and to estimate where fish will be feeding. Many other people watch the weather for warnings of tornadoes, hurricanes and floods. Predicting the weather accurately can help to save crops, livestock and human lives.

Today, scientists know a great deal about the conditions that influence weather. Modern instruments help them predict the weather more accurately than ever before.   However, it is important to remember that, though scientists know much more about the weather, they cannot control the weather. God is still in control of whether the sky is sunny or cloudy, the clouds will release or hold rain, or the breeze will blow or be still.

Who covers the heavens with clouds, Who prepares rain for the earth, Who makes grass to grow on the mountain ... He gives snow like wool; He scatters the frost like ashes. He casts out His hail like morsels; Who can stand before His cold? He sends out His word and melts them; He causes His wind to blow, and the waters flow.

Psalm 147:8, 16-18

Section 8-1: Composition of the Atmosphere

What materials make up this bubble that surrounds the earth? As I said before, the atmosphere is made up of a mixture of gases. What are these gases? The gases that make up the earth's atmosphere include nitrogen, oxygen, carbon dioxide, water vapor, argon, and trace gases. About 78 percent of the atmosphere is nitrogen, 21 percent is oxygen, and the remaining 1 percent is a combination of the other gases mentioned. Color and label the graph below.

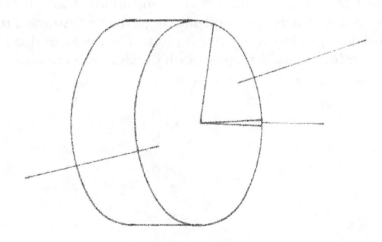

Nitrogen: The most abundant gas in the atmosphere, nitrogen, is needed by living things to make proteins. Plants use nitrogen combined with other chemicals to make plant proteins. Animals need proteins for the growth and repair of body parts. Animals get the proteins they need by eating plants.

Nitrogen is returned to the atmosphere when dead animals and plants decay. This continual movement of nitrogen is called the nitrogen cycle.

Oxygen: The second most abundant gas in the atmosphere, oxygen, is used directly from the atmosphere by most plants and animals. It is used for respiration where living things chemically combine oxygen with food and use it for energy.

Carbon Dioxide: Though the amount of carbon dioxide in the atmosphere is very small, it is very important. Carbon dioxide is used by plants during the food-making process. Animals return carbon dioxide into the air by respiration. The decay of dead plants and animals also returns carbon dioxide into the air.

Section 8-2: Layers of the Atmosphere

Now we will travel through the earth's atmosphere and explore its different layers. As we soar up from the surface of the earth to the high edge of outer space, we will notice many changes in the atmosphere. The atmosphere is divided into layers according to the differences in temperature.

The layers of the earth's atmosphere are held close to the earth by the force of gravity. We learned about gravity in Chapter 1. The layers of the atmosphere being drawn towards the earth create what is called **air pressure**. The upper layers push down on the lower layers, so air pressure is greater in the lower layers. You may have felt your ears "pop" if you have ever flown in an airplane. This is because of the change in air pressure.

Let's begin our journey through the invisible part of the earth — Earth's atmosphere.

Troposphere: We begin our journey without moving an inch. The layer of atmosphere in which we live is called the troposphere. Almost all of Earth's weather occurs in the troposphere. We will learn more about weather in the following sections. The height of the troposphere varies. At the equator, it is about 17 kilometers; at the poles, it is about 7 kilometers. Between these areas, the troposphere extends about 12 kilometers.

Stratosphere: As we continue past the troposphere, we notice a drop in temperature. In fact, we must move indoors because the temperature drops to -60 degrees Celsius. Winds whip past our ship, making a whistling sound. Here very strong eastward winds blow horizontally around the earth. These **jet streams** can reach speeds of more than 320 kilometers per hour. Through our vents, we can smell a clean, sharp smell.

It smells like we just had a thunderstorm — like electricity has just broken the air. This odor comes from **ozone**, a special form of oxygen. Ozone acts as a shield for the earth's surface. Without it, the sun's harmful ultraviolet radiation would reach the earth's surface and would burn our bodies.

As we move to the upper layer of the stratosphere, our temperature gauges record an increase in temperature. It is 18 degrees Celsius. As ultraviolet radiation reacts with ozone, heat is given off.

Mesosphere: Our temperature gauges begin to drop again as we continue moving away from the earth. It is now -100 degrees Celsius. This drop marks the beginning of the mesosphere, which extends about 30 kilometers beyond the stratosphere. We see a bright flash. Then another. Bright streaks of fire whiz through the air like shooting stars. It is like watching a fireworks show. Can you guess what is going on? We are experiencing a meteor shower. The mesosphere helps protect the earth from meteoroids — the large rocks in space that we learned about in Chapter One. Meteoroids burn up in the mesosphere because of the friction between the meteoroid and the atmosphere. We call these burning meteoroids "shooting stars."

Thermosphere: The ship's gauges show that we are now in an area where the air is very thin. The density of the atmosphere and the air pressure are only about one ten-millionth of what they are at the earth's surface. Also, the temperature gauge shows a dramatic change. The temperature reading reaches almost 2000 degrees Celsius! The temperature to melt steel into a liquid is about 1900 degrees Celsius. Fortunately our ship is made of materials that cannot be melted at this high temperature. Thermosphere means "warm layer." The nitrogen and oxygen in the thermosphere absorb a great deal of the ultraviolet radiation from space.

There is no definite upper limit to the thermosphere. The lower thermosphere is called the **ionosphere**. The ionosphere extends from 80 kilometers to 550 kilometers above the earth's surface. Electrically charged particles in the ionosphere called ions are used for radio communication. AM radio waves are bounced off the ions and back to the Earth's surface.

The upper thermosphere is called the **exosphere** extends from about 550 kilometers above the earth's surface for thousands of kilometers. It is in the exosphere that artificial satellites orbit the earth. These satellites are used in television transmission and telephone communication. They are also used to gather information on the world's weather, as we will learn in the next sections.

Each layer of the atmosphere is represented in the diagram on the right. Write the name of the layer in the correct spot.

We have completed our trip through the atmosphere. Now we will return to the troposphere layer where weather takes place, and we will study the weather in more detail.

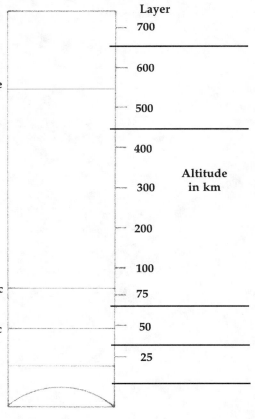

229

Section 8-3: Weather

We have learned about the earth's atmosphere, its composition, and the layers of the earth's atmosphere. However, we haven't discussed the daily condition of earth's atmosphere. Perhaps you didn't know it, but you have probably been studying the daily condition of the Earth's atmosphere all your life. Have you ever waked up in the morning and looked out the window to see if it was rainy or sunny? What you were trying to determine was the **weather**. The weather is the daily condition of the earth's atmosphere.

Draw a picture of your favorite type of weather. Include a drawing of yourself with the correct type of clothes needed for the weather.

Section 8-4: The Causes of Weather

Weather affects our daily lives and influences our environment. We dress ourselves according to the weather. We build our homes to withstand the extremities of the weather. Our leisure activities are determined by the weather. Perhaps you ice skate on a frozen pond during the winter, and cool off at the lake during the summer.

What determines what our weather will be? The **heat** from the sun causes the air to warm up. The heating of the air causes it to move, and as the air moves, **winds** are formed. Clouds are formed when a lot of moisture from the air collects in the sky. When the clouds can no longer hold all this **moisture**, it falls to earth as rain, hail, or snow. Thus, the three factors that determine our weather are heat, winds, and moisture. Let's learn more about heat, winds, and moisture.

Heat: Almost all of the earth's energy comes from the sun. This energy is called radiant energy. As the sun's rays reach the atmosphere, part of the energy is bounced back into space, and part of it is scattered throughout the atmosphere. Some of this energy in the atmosphere reaches the earth's surface. Here it is absorbed by the earth and changed into heat. This is the heat we feel, called **air temperature**.

Air temperature is measured by a thermometer. Most thermometers consist of a thin glass tube with a bulb at one end. The bulb is filled with a liquid that expands when it is hot, or contracts when it is cool. When it expands, the liquid will move up the tube, and the temperature will be higher. When it contracts, the liquid will move down the tube, and the temperature will be lower.

Winds: What causes the wind to blow? Winds are formed by the movement of air from one place to another. When air is heated, the warm air rises. The cooler air moves in underneath the rising warm air. This movement of air is the wind.

For example, during the day, the air over a land area is often warmer than the air over a nearby lake or sea. The air is warmer because the land heats up faster than the water. As the warm air over the land rises, the cooler air over the sea moves inland to take its place. This flow of air from the sea to the land is called a **sea breeze**.

During the night, the land cools off faster than the water. The air over the sea is now warmer than the air over the land. This warm air over the sea rises. The cooler air over the land moves to replace the rising warm air over the sea. A flow of air from the land to the sea is called a **land breeze**.

The name of a wind tells you from which direction the wind is blowing. A land breeze blows from the land to the sea. A sea breeze blows from the sea to the land. A west wind blows from the west to the east. A south wind blows from the south to the north.

Which diagram below illustrates a land breeze? Which one illustrates a sea breeze?

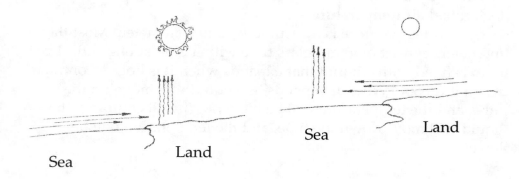

Moisture: Have you ever noticed how the air can sometimes feel damp? You may have heard someone describe this condition as "humid." That means that there is a lot of moisture in the air. At any given time, the atmosphere holds about 14 million tons of moisture! Winds carry this moisture all over the earth.

Sometimes the moisture in the air mixes with small particles of dust or other solids in the air to form clouds. Clouds come in all sorts of shapes and sizes. The three main types of clouds are cumulus, stratus, and cirrus clouds.

Cumulus clouds look like piles of cotton balls in the sky. These clouds are fluffy and white with flat bottoms. They form at middle altitudes. Cumulus clouds usually indicate fair weather. However, when cumulus clouds get larger and darker on the bottom, they produce thunderstorms. These large thunderclouds are called cumulonimbus clouds.

Smooth, gray clouds that cover the whole sky and block out the sun are called stratus clouds. They form at low altitudes. Light rain and drizzle are usually associated with stratus clouds. Nimbostratus clouds bring rain and snow. When stratus clouds form close to the ground, the result is fog.

Feathery clouds are called cirrus clouds. Cirrus clouds form at very high altitudes. Cirrus clouds are made of ice crystals. You can see cirrus clouds in fair weather, but they often indicate that rain or snow will fall within several hours.

Clouds can fall to the earth in the form of rain, sleet, snow, or hail. Water that falls from the atmosphere to the earth is called precipitation. Before water falls to the earth as precipitation, cloud droplets must get bigger by colliding and combining with other droplets. When the droplets get too heavy for the cloud to hold they fall down to the earth as rain. When falling raindrops pass through an extremely cold layer of air, they freeze into small ice pellets called sleet. Another form of precipitation, snow, forms when water vapor freezes. Snowflakes are flat, six-sided ice crystals that have beautiful shapes. No two snowflakes are exactly alike.

Hail is one of the most damaging forms of precipitation. It is usually formed in cumulonimbus clouds. Hailstones are balls or chunks of ice. Hailstones are formed when water droplets hit ice pellets in a cloud and freeze. If the upward wind is strong enough, the hailstones can stay in the cloud and get bigger and bigger, until the heaviness makes them fall to the ground. One of the largest hailstones ever found fell on Coffeyville, Kansas, in September 1970. This hailstone measured 140 millimeters in diameter!

Activity: Label three of the different types of clouds and three of the different types of precipitation.

Activity: Weather Observations

Materials: paper, pencils, and the provided chart.

Procedure: For several weeks, watch on television or read in a newspaper the weather predictions for the following day. Record these predictions in the chart below. Then observe the actual weather. Note whether it is sunny, windy, or rainy weather, and whether it is cold, warm, or hot. Record these observations on the chart below. Compare the predictions with the actual weather.

date	weather prediction	actual weather

Activity:
What Type of Weather Do I Like?

Read each word in the following list and discuss it with other students or your teacher. Decide how you feel about that type of weather and write the word under the proper heading.

Word List:

warm	freezing	clear	rainy
cool	icy	fair	stormy
breezy	chilly	balmy	humid
drizzly	hot	windy	cloudy
overcast	hazy	cold	wet
foggy	sunny		

<u>Types of weather I like</u>   <u>Types of weather I dislike</u>

Activity:
Creating a Rain Gauge

Materials: rulers, glass jars with straight sides and flat bottoms, tape or rubber bands

Procedure:

1. Place the ruler in the jar.

2. Wrap the rubber band around the ruler twice and then around the edge of the jar; or use a durable tape to attach the ruler to the inside of the jar.

3. If rainfall is predicted, place the rain gauge in an open area for collection.

4. Check the gauge every day it rains and record the amount of rainfall in inches or centimeters.

Section 8-5: Changes in the Weather

The sight of a tornado is an awesome thing. This violent storm can hurl heavy objects hundreds of meters, destroy bridges and buildings, and kill people and livestock. Perhaps you have seen a tornado on television or experienced the effects of one in real life. What forces brought about this tornado? Write your guesses on the lines below.

_____

_____

_____

_____

_____.

Good work! Now let's check to see if your answer(s) are correct. Our ship is destined for the North Pole where we will see one of the biggest traffic jams ever!

We have arrived at the top of our atmosphere near the North Pole. Much of our weather conditions and changes are associated with the movement of **air masses**. Air masses are large bodies of air that have taken on the temperature and humidity of a part of the earth's surface. Because we usually cannot see air, we will need to look through a special window of our ship to see the cause of our weather changes.

As you look down, you will see that the regions around the North Pole are covered by a huge cold air mass. This cap of dense air pushes slowly southward. The earth's rotation twists the cold air mass so that it moves from east to west, forming the winds called the polar easterlies.

Cold Front

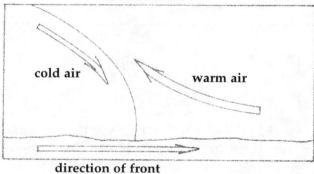

direction of front

Warm Front

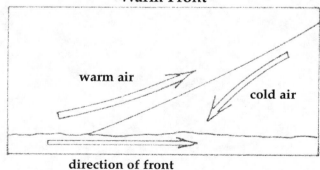

direction of front

Now we must look south. As the polar easterlies are moving south, warm moist air masses are moving northward toward the North Pole. This air generally moves from west to east, forming the winds called the westerlies. The polar easterlies and the westerlies cause the air masses to meet and move past each other, like traffic on opposite sides of a highway. When two air masses that have different properties meet, they do not mix easily. The boundary where the cold air meets the warm air is called the **polar front**. The weather at a front is usually unsettled and stormy.

When different fronts collide, storms occur. Let's get closer to the surface of the earth and learn about the different types of storms. We are at the North Pole now. As we travel toward the equator, the ship's storm tracking system will lead us to each type of storm. Your job is to guess what type of storm we are experiencing. At the end, the correct answers will be given. Adventures are often dangerous, but I'm sure our trustworthy ship can weather it all!

A. Heavy rain is falling over us. However, as it touches our ship, the trees, the power lines and other surfaces, the rain instantly freezes. Everything is covered in a layer of glittering ice. Long icicles hang from the overhangs of houses. Everywhere we look, we see long, snowy, pointed beards. What kind of storm is this?

_____.

Good guess!

B. It is no longer raining and freezing. A muffled quietude surrounds us. One little snowflake silently floats down and lands on the ship's deck. Soon another follows. Then another. The snow falls faster and thicker. The ship's deck is covered in a thin blanket of snow. The air is filled with light, fluffy snowflakes. What kind of storm is this?

_____.

C. A heavy snowfall is falling down on us. The winds are beginning to pick up. Soon the snow is no longer falling, but blowing at us at a wind speed of more than 56 kilometers per hour. The temperature is below -7 degrees Celsius. We are having trouble guiding our ship. The hard-blown snow blinds us and makes it almost impossible to see. What kind of storm are we experiencing?

_____.

D. Whew! We made it through! Now the winds have died
down. The air is warming up. It feels heavy and damp. Sounds
are muffled, as if we were in a cave. The clouds are low, thick, and
dark. We hear a drip, drip, drop! Then more — dibble, dibble,
dopp, dopp! A steady rainfall is now under way. What kind of
storm is this?

_____.

E. The rain has stopped, but the air still feels warm, moist,
and heavy. At the horizon, a crooked streak of light pierces the
darkness and zaps the ground. In the distance we hear a low rumble, like a gigantic stomach growling.
  Soon after, we see a thin curve of black smoke. Minutes
later, a small bonfire lights up. What kind of storm is this?

_____.

F. We have passed through that storm. Wet and dripping,
we travel on to a distant coast. We see a mighty ocean. The air is
calm and serene. Would you believe we are in the middle of a
storm? We are in what is called the eye of a storm. As the eye
moves onward, the winds pick up, eventually reaching speeds of
200 kilometers per hour. It also begins to rain heavily.
  High waves form and crash onto the beach, flooding many
of the coastal buildings. Strong winds cause some buildings to
sway; other buildings crumble and fall. As the rain continues,
serious flooding occurs in other parts of the region. In terms of
total energy involved, this is the most powerful storm we have or
will ever experience. This type of storm is the most powerful
storm on Earth! What is it?

_____.

245

   G. We have passed through yet another storm! Now, as we look around, we see we are in the middle of a vast plain. It is late afternoon or early evening. We see low, heavy cumulonimbus clouds. Winds are picking up. Our ship's gauge shows us that the air pressure is extremely low. We look up at the cabin roof, and it seems to be breathing, bending up and down, up and down. We look out the window and see a whirling, black funnel. The winds have reached speeds of more than 350 kilometers per hour. Roofs and walls of buildings are blown out by the winds. A railroad car is picked up and thrown hundreds of meters. What kind of storm is this?

_____.

Wow! That was an adventure. Now for the answers. As you correct your guesses, read the information about each storm to learn more about our weather system.

A. Ice Storm: An ice storm covers everything in its path, like frosting on a cake or glaze on a doughnut. Although it may look beautiful, an ice storm can cause serious damage by knocking down trees and power lines.

B. Snowstorm: When two different fronts collide during the winter, a snowstorm usually develops. A heavy snowfall occurs.

C. Blizzard: A blizzard is a snowstorm that has a wind speed of more than 56 kilometers per hour, and the temperature is below 7 degrees Celsius.

D. Rainstorm: When a warm front moves in and meets a cold front, heavy nimbostratus clouds develop. In the summer, the result is a steady rainfall that lasts for several hours.

E. Thunderstorm: When a cold front moves in and meets a warm front, cumulonimbus clouds produce thunderstorms. Thunderstorms are heavy rainstorms accompanied by thunder and lightning. These storms can be quite dangerous. During a thunderstorm, areas of positive and negative electric charges build up in storm clouds. Lightning is a sudden discharge, or spark, of electricity between two clouds or between a cloud and the ground.
Lightning striking the ground is the leading cause of forest fires in the western states. Lightning may also strike people, animals, or buildings. In fact, more people are killed every year by lightning than as a result of any other violent storm!

Safety tips:
1) Avoid open spaces, but do not take shelter under a tree.
2) The best shelter is inside a building.
3) Stay away from sinks, bathtubs, televisions, and telephones.

Lightning is usually followed by loud thunderclaps. The electrical discharge of lightning heats up the air. When the air is heated, it expands rapidly and results in sound waves. Although lightning and thunder occur at the same time, we see lightning first and then hear the thunder. This is because light travels much faster than sound. If you hear thunder about three seconds after you see a flash of lightning, the lightning is about one kilometer away.

Discussion: How can you tell if a thunderstorm is moving toward or away from you?

F. Hurricanes: A hurricane is a powerful storm that forms over tropical oceans. Hurricanes that form over the western Pacific Ocean are called typhoons. During late summer and early autumn, low-pressure areas often form over the Caribbean or the Gulf of Mexico. Warm, moist air begins to rise rapidly. Cooler air moves in, and the air begins to spin. This process forms what is called a cyclone (a low-pressure area containing rising warm air).

The fast-spinning, rising air forms a circular wall of strong winds, clouds, and rainfall. Inside the wall, the air is calm. This was the eye of the storm we experienced. Outside the eye, winds may reach speeds between 120 and 320 kilometers per hour.

The high waves and strong winds of a hurricane often cause severe damage. A typical hurricane lasts for about nine days. Sometimes it can last for as long as three to four weeks. Coastal areas are usually hardest hit by hurricanes. As a hurricane moves inland, it loses its force and power.

G. Tornadoes: A tornado is a whirling, funnel-shaped cloud that develops in low, heavy, cumulonimbus clouds. The air pressure at the bottom of the funnel is extremely low. When this funnel of low air pressure touches the ground, it acts like a giant vacuum cleaner.

Meteorologists are still not sure how tornadoes are formed. They believe that tornadoes are formed when, for unknown reasons, fast-moving cold air rides up over warm, moist air. The warm air rises rapidly, creating an area of very low pressure. Air rushes in from the sides of the low-pressure area, giving the rising column of air a twisting motion.

Safety tip: The safest place to be during a tornado is in a basement or under something strong enough to support a heavy load.

More tornadoes occur in the United States than in any other country in the world. They are most common on the Great Plains, which is often called Tornado Alley. Here, cool, dry air from the west collides with warm, moist air from the Gulf of Mexico. Tornadoes usually occur in spring during the late afternoon or early evening.

A tornado may measure no more than one kilometer across, but tornadoes can produce the strongest winds on Earth — winds that may travel more than 650 kilometers per hour!

Section 8-6: Climate

We have learned about air masses, the fronts between them, and the storms connected with the fronts. These are the main causes of weather changes. However, now we will learn about climate. Climate is the average weather at a particular place. The climate of an area is determined by the air masses that are associated with its location on the earth's surface.

For example, the climate of regions near the equator is the result of warm air masses. The average temperature during the year is 18 degrees Celsius and above. This climate zone is called tropical.

On the other hand, air masses formed near the poles determine the climate zone called polar. Average yearly temperature for regions with a polar climate is 10 degrees Celsius or less. The summers are short, and the winters are long and harsh.

Between the equator and the poles are regions with temperate climates. This kind of climate is affected by both warm and cold air masses. The weather in the temperate climatic regions is very different from day to day and from one part of the year to another. Most of the United States is located in this region.

Complete the illustration below by labeling the appropriate regions with their corresponding climate zones.

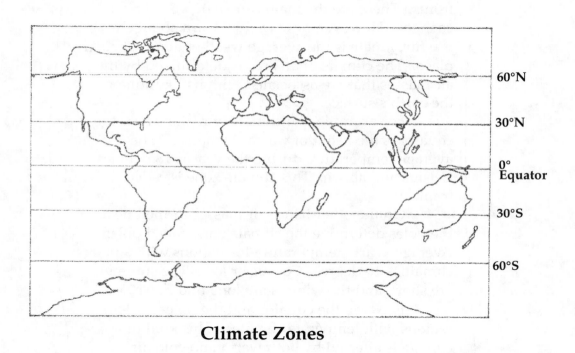

Climate Zones

Section 3-5:   Predicting the Weather

Mankind has tried to predict the weather for centuries. In Matthew, Jesus points out how the people knew how to predict the weather fairly accurately, yet they failed to understand the meaning of Christ's arrival. "When evening comes, you say, 'It will be fair weather, for the sky is red,' and in the morning, 'Today it will be stormy, for the sky is red and overcast.' You know how to interpret the appearance of the sky, but you cannot interpret the signs of the times." Matthew 16:2-4

Today we have much more complex ways of interpreting the weather. Though our knowledge has increased about the weather, people still are missing the point about Jesus' coming to Earth to die for our sins. Though weather predictions have become more and more accurate, God still reminds us of just who controls the weather. Learning about how to predict the weather should make us amazed at God's wonderful creation, not puffed up with man's knowledge.

As we learn about the different instruments man uses to predict the weather, think about how God still has the whole world in His hands.

Rain Gauge: One of the simplest weather instruments used by meteorologists is the rain gauge. A rain gauge can be any container with straight sides, like a jar. The gauge is used to collect and measure the amount of rain that has fallen in a particular area.

Wind Vane: A wind vane is turned by the wind so that it points into the wind. You may remember that winds are named for the direction from which they come. For example, a wind blowing from south to north is called a south wind.

Anemometer: This instrument is used to measure wind speed.

Weather Satellites: These instruments in space send television pictures that are used to follow cloud movements. They also follow warm and cool currents.

Radar: Rain, snow, and the location of air masses can be detected with radar.

Weather Balloon: Instruments can be sent up in weather balloons. The airborne instruments gather information at different levels in the atmosphere and send the data by radio to stations on the ground.

Weather Maps: In the United States, information about weather is gathered from more than 300 local weather stations. These stations provide information about temperature, air pressure, precipitation, and wind speed and direction. All this data is used to prepare a daily weather map. A weather map is like a photograph of local weather conditions.

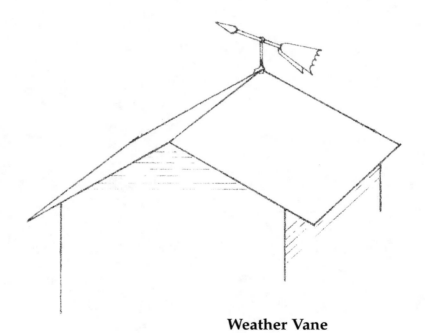

Weather Vane

EARTH'S ATMOSPHERE

Chapter 8 Review

1. Define atmosphere.

2. In which layer of the atmosphere do jet streams occur?

3. What purpose does the ozone layer serve?

4. The mesosphere helps to shield the earth from what danger?

5. The ionosphere and exonosphere are the lower and upper parts of which layer of the atmosphere? In a paragraph, compare these two parts.

6. What is weather?

7. What three factors work together to determine what our weather will be?

8. What is the earth's main source of energy?

9. In a paragraph, summarize what causes the wind to blow.

10. Name three things that can fall from the clouds.

11. Define air masses and polar front.

12. List one safety tip that you should follow in a lightning storm.

13. What is climate? List the different climate zones.

14. Describe the function of three instruments that scientists use to predict the weather.

Student Objectives
Chapter 9: Earth's Moon

My objectives are:

1. I will draw the moon in all its phases.

2. I will demonstrate the moon in all its phases using an activity.

3. I will test whether the moon is larger when it appears on the horizon than when it is higher in the sky.

4. I will complete a cross section of the moon.

5. I will complete a diagram of the moon's effect on Earth's tides.

Chapter 9 — Earth's Moon

A satellite is a body moving in orbit around a larger body. We have many satellites orbiting the earth. As we discussed in the previous chapter, we have satellites that tell us about the weather, help us see television, and communicate on telephones. However, all these satellites are artificial satellites. They are man-made.

We also have a natural satellite — the moon. The moon was not made by man, but by God. Genesis 1:14-19 reads, "Then God said, 'Let there be lights...' Then God made two great lights; the greater light to rule the day, and the lesser light to rule the night; He made the stars also." God designed the moon to give us light.

In the past, astronauts have landed on the moon to explore our nearest neighbor in space. We, too, shall travel to the moon and learn about this interesting satellite — God's special satellite which He created for us.

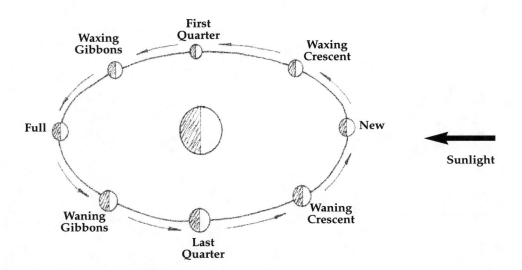

Section 9-1: Phases of the Moon

Before we travel to the moon, let's first examine it right from right where we are. Sometimes the moon is a gigantic fingernail clipping in the sky. Sometimes it is a half-circle. Sometimes it seems to be a glowing pearl, perfect and whole. We can see the moon only because the moon reflects light from the sun. The position of the moon, the earth, and the sun determine how the moon appears to us in the sky. The different changes in the appearance of the moon to us on Earth are called the **moon's phases**.

If you would note the appearance of the moon every day, you would see a pattern. If each day, more and more of the moon becomes lighted, you are watching a **waxing** moon. If the moon becomes darker each day, you are witnessing a **waning** moon. Let's examine the many faces of the moon more closely. Look at the diagram on page 266 and then read about each phase.

New Moon: When the moon is between the earth and the sun, we see no moon at all, or perhaps only a faint outline. This is because only the shaded side, the dark side, of the moon is facing us. The other side of the moon is brilliantly lit, but there is no one over there to see it! How many brilliant full moons we have missed! If we were standing on the dark side of the moon during this phase, we could see the sunlit side of the earth.

Crescent: As the moon moves in its orbit, a small part of its lighted side appears. This is when the moon looks like a gigantic fingernail clipping. This is the crescent phase.

First and Last Quarters: When the moon has moved one quarter of the way through its orbit, one half of its bright side is visible. This phase is called the first quarter. (This phase is when the moon is waxing.) When the moon has moved three-quarters of the way through its orbit, the other half of its bright side is visible. This phase is called the last quarter. (This phase occurs when the moon is waning.)

Gibbous: When the moon has moved further in its orbit, we begin to see a football-shaped moon. This is the gibbous phase.

Full Moon: The amount of sunlight keeps increasing until all of the sunlit side of the moon can be seen from the earth. The fully-lit side of the moon is called the full moon.

It takes 29 1/2 days for the moon to complete a full cycle.

New	Waxing Crescent	First Quarter	Waxing Gibbons
Full	Waning Crescent	Last Quarter	Waning Gibbons

Activity: In the squares below, list and draw the different phases of the moon.

Activity: Phases of the mMon

Materials: flashlight, ball, tape, and three index cards labeled Earth, sun, and moon

Procedure:
1. Tape the card labeled Earth on your chest, tape the card labeled moon on the ball, and tape the sun card to another person.

2. The person with the sun card should hold a flashlight so that your entire body is illuminated.

3. Hold the ball at arm's length above your head and in front of you, and face the sun. From this position, the side of the ball that you see should not be lit. This position represents a new moon.

4. Slowly rotate your body counterclockwise until you reach a 90-degree turn. As you move, the light should create a crescent shape, like the shape of a fingernail clipping and then grow to light up half of the moon. This is the first-quarter position.

5. Continue rotating another 90 degrees. You may have to bend your head so as to avoid an eclipse. The light should illuminate the entire side which you are facing. This position represents a full moon.

6. Continue rotating another 90 degrees. The moon will be in the third quarter position. Another 90 degrees will place the ball back to its original position.

Questions

1. During a new moon, does a person on Earth see the dark or light side of the moon?

2. During a full moon, does a person on Earth see the dark or light side of the moon?

3. How many full moons occur in one year?

4. How many months are in one year?

Activity: Is the moon larger at the horizon?

People often exclaim at how large the moon is when it is near the horizon. When it is higher in the sky, it appears smaller. Is the moon really closer to the earth when it appears at the horizon or is this an illusion? Compare the moon with a dime held at arm's length when the moon is near the horizon and later when the moon is high in the sky. Write your observation on the lines below.

_____

_____

_____

_____

_____.

Section 9-2: The Moon's Characteristics

Before we journey to the moon, let's learn some interesting facts about this place. To reach the moon, we will have to travel about 384,403 kilometers from Earth. The moon is about one fourth the diameter of Earth, 3476 kilometers. The distance around the moon is about 10,927 kilometers. The surface area is about 37,943,000 square kilometers. The moon's crust is about 60 kilometers thick. The central core is thought to be made of melted iron.

We have landed on the moon. Zip up your special space suits, and let's get out of the ship. Before we begin moonwalking, let's examine the moon right from where we are. Note the quietness of the place. There are no winds, no storms, no rain, and no clouds. Because the moon has no atmosphere, there is no weather. The moon is a dry, airless, and barren world. Reach down and touch the moon's surface. It is hard and rocky. A test of a moon rock shows no signs of water. Scientists believe that there never was any water on the moon.

It is night. Our temperature gauge shows us that the surface temperature of the moon is -175 degrees Celsius. During the day, temperatures may rise above 100 degrees Celsius. Fortunately our space suits protect us from these extreme temperatures.

As we begin to walk, we notice that our steps do not feel as if we were on Earth. We bounce high into the air, and it takes a long time for us to land again. It feels like those dreams in which you can only move in slow motion. The moon's gravity is only one sixth that of the earth. Objects weigh less on the moon than they do on Earth. Divide your weight by 6. What do you actually weigh right now, standing on the moon? _____.

The ground below us begins to shake and tremble. We feel it again and again. This is not an earthquake, though it feels like one. Remember, we're not on Earth; we're on the moon. We're experiencing a moonquake. Astronauts who have visited before us left instruments to measure these moonquakes. As many as 3,000 moonquakes have been recorded per year.

We wait until the moonquake has stopped. Then we continue. We are crossing broad, smooth, lowland plains. These are called **maria**, which is the Latin word for seas. This name was given by the first person to look at the moon through a telescope — Galileo in 1609. Galileo saw dark and light areas on the moon and named the dark areas "maria". We know now that there is no water on the moon. The maria are filled with hardened rock that may be the result of volcanic activity.

As we reach the edge of the plain, we come to one of the most striking features of the moon — a crater. The moon's surface is covered with craters of all sizes. Some are hundreds of meters across. Scientists believe the craters were formed from meteoroids hitting the surface of the moon.

Up ahead we see a mountain range that soars thousands of meters into the black sky. This is called a **highland**. Some of the highlands on the moon reach eight kilometers above the surrounding plains. As we reach the top of one of these high places and look down at the area that stretches out before us, we see a pattern of long valleys that crisscross the surface. These valleys are called rilles. Rilles may be the result of past volcanic activity, or are cracks formed by moonquakes. Scientists are still guessing at what the moon was like before they began to explore it.

Now we will travel back to the earth and learn about one of the interesting effects the moon has on Earth.

Section 9-3: Tides

The moon is so close to the earth that there is a gravitational attraction between the earth and the moon. The Earth's pull on the moon has resulted in a distinct bulge on the side of the moon facing the earth. However, the moon also pulls on the earth. The result of this pull is the rise and fall of the oceans as the moon moves in its orbit around the earth.

Let's visit the beach! We have reached the beach, and we have marked the level of the ocean at the shoreline. Every hour we mark the level of the ocean. What do we find? The ocean appears to be breathing! The ocean level rises on the beach for about six hours. Then the ocean level falls for another six hours. The rise and fall of the oceans as a result of the moon's gravitational pull are called **tides**.

Now we will have to do some fast traveling. As the ocean reaches high tide here, we will travel to the opposite side of the earth and measure the ocean tide there. We find that on the opposite side of the earth, it is also high tide. Let's travel just a quarter of the way around the earth. Here we find that it is low tide. On the opposite side of the earth, it is also low tide. We have found that, at any given time, two places are experiencing high tide, and at the same time, two places are experiencing low tide. What is happening?

As the moon's gravity pulls on the earth, it causes the oceans to bulge. The oceans bulge in two places: on the side of the earth facing the moon and on the side of the earth facing away from the moon. At the same time, the bulging at the two sides causes low tides in the places between the two bulges. Look at the diagram below.

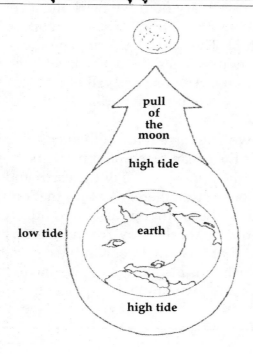

There are many more interesting facts about tides. For example, because the moon rises about 50 minutes later each day, the high and the low tides at a given place are also 50 minutes later each day. High tides are higher during the full moon and the new moon phases than at other times. These higher tides are called **spring tides**. The reason for this is because the sun and the moon are in a direct line with the earth. When the moon is at the first and last quarter phases, the sun interferes with the moon's gravitational pull. This results in lower tides called **neap tides**.

Chapter 9 Review

1. What is a satellite?

2. How many natural satellites does the earth have?

3. Define waxing and waning.

4. How far is the moon from the Earth?

5. Describe the moon's maria, highlands, and rilles.

6. Why do tides occur?

Unit Three

God's Handiwork

Three
3

Student Objectives
Chapter 10: Basic Building Blocks

My objectives are:

1) I will decode a message of listed elements using the periodic table of elements.

2) I will draw a diagram of an atom and label its major parts.

3) I will draw a prokaryotic cell.

4) I will label the major organelles in an animal and a plant cell.

5) I will create a poster that lists the three main points of the cell theory and include a drawing of an animal or a plant cell.

Chapter 10: Basic Building Blocks

In this chapter, we will be learning about Earth's matter. What is matter? **Matter** is anything that takes up space and has mass. So really, we have been studying matter all along. However, it is in this chapter that we will be exploring the three basic forms of matter: elements, compounds and mixtures, and the basic building blocks of all matter — atoms.

We will also study the basic building blocks of living things: cells. As we explore atoms and cells, we will marvel at their complexity. God has intricately designed even the smallest things known to man. Ralph Waldo Emerson wrote, "Nature is too thin a screen, the glory of the One breaks in everywhere." Notice how the glory of God breaks through the small parts of nature.

Section 10-1: Elements, Compounds, and Mixtures

We are up in the volcanic mountains of an equatorial country. We are surrounded by rainforest. Clouds appear to be forming around our feet, and rising into the air. We climb to the summit of the volcano that is before us. We reach its crater, and look down into the pit. A brilliant, yellow eye appears to stare back at us. The bottom of the crater is covered with a yellow, bubbling liquid. The smell of rotten eggs wafts through the air. What are we seeing?

We are looking at sulfur, a type of matter that smells like rotten eggs and has a yellow color. Sulfur is an element. Keep reading to learn about elements and other forms of matter.

All matter can be classified into three forms: elements, compounds, and mixtures. An **element** is a substance that cannot be separated into simpler substances. It is in its simplest form. Some examples of elements are easily recognizable — oxygen, gold, sodium, and many more. So far, scientists have identified 109 elements; 90 of these elements occur naturally. All the elements that have been identified are listed in a chart called the **periodic table of the elements** found on page 420.

Understanding the periodic table of the elements is like decoding a message. In order to understand it, you must know the code. Each element is represented by a symbol of one or two letters. Some symbols are the same as the first letter of the name of the element. For instance, the symbol for carbon is C, for oxygen O, for sulfur S, and for hydrogen H. Other elements that begin with the same letter must add a letter to the symbol to prevent confusion. For example, the symbol for helium is He; for chlorine, Cl; and for silicon, Si. Other elements have symbols that are related to their Latin names. The important thing is that you must know the code in order to understand the symbols.

A **compound** is made of different elements that are chemically bonded together. The chemically combined substance has a different set of properties from the separate elements. For example, hydrogen and oxygen are usually gases. However, when the two are combined in a certain manner, they form water.

A **mixture** is two or more substances mixed together, but each substance retains its own properties. Because the substances that make up a mixture are not chemically combined, they can be separated by physical means. For instance, we learned about salt water in the chapter on oceans. Salt water is a mixture of water and salt. The sun's heat causes pure water to separate from the salt water by evaporation. Compounds can only be separated chemically.

Activity: Decode a message between two friends using the Periodic Table of Elements found on page 420.

Phosphorus Aluminum,

Tungsten Helium Rhenium   Tungsten Arsenic

Chlorine Arsenic Sulfur?

Nobelium Oxygen Neon   Argon Oxygen Uranium Neodymium.

Iodine   Americium   Astatine   Lithium Bromine Argon Yttrium.

Calcium Nitrogen   Yttrium Oxygen Uranium   Beryllium

Astatine   Scandium Iodine - Fluorine Iodine

Selenium Carbon Titanium Oxygen Nitrogen   Astatine

Nitrogen Iodine Neon?

                                Krypton Yttrium Sulfur Titanium

Section 10-2: The Atom

As we discussed in the introduction, atoms are the building blocks of matter. An **atom** is the smallest part of an element that has all the properties of that element. We will explore the atom and learn about its structure.

We have shrunk down to the size of one of the smallest things known to man — an atom. What will we find? The atom is before us. Whirling around the outer part of the structure are particles with a negative charge. These are called **electrons.** These electrons are given away, added to, or shared to form **molecules.** A molecule is two or more atoms held together by chemical forces.

At the center of the atom, we find what is called the **nucleus.** The nucleus houses two different kinds of particles: protons and neutrons. A **proton** is a positively charged particle. A **neutron** has no charge. It is a neutral particle. Look at the diagram below. Label all the atom's major parts.

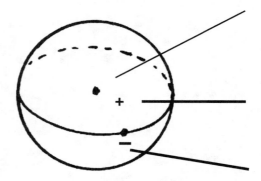

Hydrogen Atom

Section 10-3: Cells

It appears that we are on another planet. Though the activities going on are similar to what we experience each day, everything looks different. Shapes and colors are softer. Things do not look as if they were built here, but as if they were grown. We arrive at a large, production plant. At the door, our identification is checked before we are allowed to enter. Once inside, we are guided to the internal highway of the plant. The highway transports us from one section of the plant to the other. It feels like we are underwater. The entire plant operates in a gel-like substance within its walls. The highway first takes us to where the product is produced, packaged, and moved to the loading docks. We watch as this department busily creates and sends out the product for the day. We are then moved to the powerhouse of the plant. This department breaks down fuel and stores it. It also supplies the entire plant with energy.

As we continue on the highway, we see several janitors clearing out discarded products, parts, and other wastes. Later, we pass the warehouses of the plant. Each warehouse stores a different type of material for the plant. We finally arrive at the center of the plant. Here, our identification is checked once again before entering. This is the control center. It is here where all the decisions are made. Important information and blueprints are stored here.

We have completed our journey through this production plant. However, we learn that we are not on another planet after all. Instead, we are in one of the basic structures that make up living things — the cell! The cell is the smallest unit of all living things, but as you can see, it is very complex. Many activities go on in this tiny unit. Lewis Thomas, an award-winning essayist, wrote about the complexity of cells:

"I have been trying to think of the earth as a kind of

organism, but it is no go. I cannot think of it this way. It is too big, too complex, with too many working parts lacking visible connections. The other night, driving through a hilly, wooded part of southern New England, I wondered about this. If not like an organism, what is (the earth) like, what is it most like? Then, satisfactorily for the moment, it came to me: it is most like a single cell."

Let's learn more about these fascinating units of life!

After many years of discovery and exploration, scientists developed one of the major theories in science — the cell theory. The cell theory summarizes the basic information about cells.

1. All organisms are made up of one or more cells.

2. Cells are the basic units of structure and function in all organisms.

3. All cells come from cells that already exist.

Let's look at each part of this theory in more depth:

1. All organisms are made of cells. In 1665, Robert Hooke, an English scientist, made a very thin slice of cork and looked at it under a microscope. The cork appeared to be made of tiny empty boxes, which he termed cells. In 1838, Matthias Schleiden, a German scientist, concluded that all plants were made of cells. A year later, another German scientist, Theodor Schwann, concluded that all animals were made up of cells. This idea has been further proven by many scientists. Cells are the basic unit of life.

• Cork cells, seen under early microscopes in the 1800's

2. Cells are the basic units of structure and function in all organisms. Living cells are dynamic, performing the necessary functions and providing structure for all living things. Though there are a variety of cells and many of them look very different and perform diverse tasks, there are certain characteristics that are common to all of them. Let's take a closer look at the organization of cells.

CELL MEMBRANE: All cells have a cell membrane. The cell membrane is the flexible, outer structure of a cell that gives it shape and regulates what enters and leaves the cell. It is made of protein and a double layer of fats.

CYTOPLASM: The gel-like material inside the cell membrane is called cytoplasm. The cytoplasm carries out the life processes in the cell.

NUCLEUS: The nucleus acts like a brain. It directs all the activities of the cell. There are two basic types of cells. Cells that have no membrane around their nuclear material are called

Animal Cell

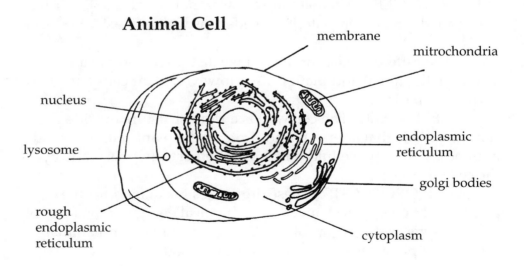

nucleus

lysosome

rough
endoplasmic
reticulum

membrane

mitrochondria

endoplasmic
reticulum

golgi bodies

cytoplasm

prokaryotic. Bacteria and cells that form pond scum are two examples. Animal and plant cells are examples of eukaryotic cells. These have a nucleus with a membrane around it. **Eukaryotic** cells also contain structures within the cytoplasm called **organelles.** Each one has a specific job. Let's explore these different "occupations" in the eukaryotic cell.

ENDOPLASMIC RETICULUM (ER): This organelle is a folded membrane that acts as the conveyor belt or internal highway for the cell. It moves materials from one place to another.

GOLGI BODIES: Golgi bodies act as the packaging plant and loading dock for proteins. Stacks of membrane-covered sacs package proteins and move them to the outside of the cell.

MITOCHONDRIA: This organelle is often called the powerhouse of the cell. The mitochondria supplies the energy demands of the cell.

LYSOSOMES: These parts of the cell are the janitors or the clean-up committee. Lysosomes contain chemicals that digest wastes, worn-out cell parts, and food.

VACUOLES: Vacuoles are the warehouses of a cell, storing water, food, and other materials needed, as well as waste products.

The different parts of the cell we just discussed are all present in both animal and plant cells. However, plant cells have two additional parts.

CELL WALL: The cell wall is a rigid structure outside the cell membrane that supports and protects the plant cell. It is made of bundles of tough cellulose fibers and other materials made by the cell.

CHLOROPLASTS: These organelles make food for the plant. Light energy is changed into chemical energy in the form of a sugar. One of the major differences between plant and animal cells is that plant cells can make their own food.

Plant Cell

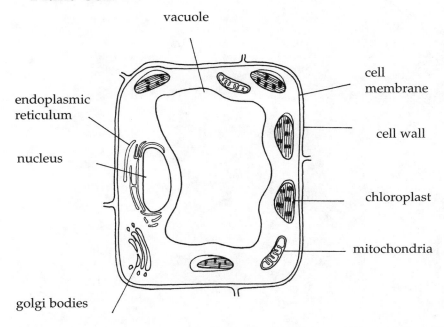

vacuole

endoplasmic
reticulum

nucleus

golgi bodies

cell
membrane

cell wall

chloroplast

mitochondria

All cells come from cells that already exist. Around 1854, a German doctor, Rudolph Virchow, hypothesized that cells divide to form new cells, rather than forming on their own. This was a revolutionary idea because many people at that time believed in the idea of "spontaneous generation" — that life comes from non-living things. For instance, people noticed that earthworms were present on the ground after a rainstorm and concluded that earthworms fell from the sky when it rained. Jan Baptist van Helmont wrote a recipe for making mice by placing grain in a corner and covering it with rags.

What Virchow argued, however, was that every cell that is or has ever been, came from a cell that already existed. In other words, living things come from other living things.

Enrichment Activity: In Madeleine L'Engle's children's book, <u>A Wind in the Door</u>, the main characters travel to the world of the cell and explore the inside of a mitochondria. Read the book and compare her descriptions of the mitochondria with what you know about cells. Is the author's interpretation correct?

Activity: Diagramming cells — Using the diagrams on pages 291 and 293, follow the directions below.

1. Prokaryotic cells have no membrane around their nuclear material and do not have organelles. Draw a prokaryotic cell in the box below.

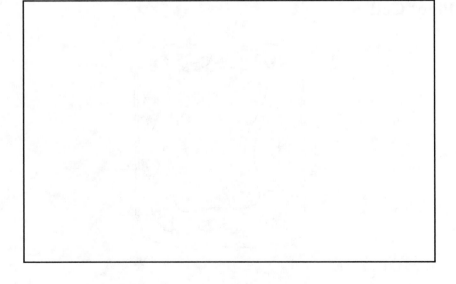

2. Eukaryotic cells have a membrane around the nucleus and also contain organelles. Plant cells have two more organelles than animal cells. Label the major organelles in the animal and plant cells below.

Animal Cell

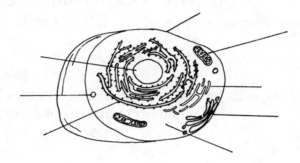

Plant Cell

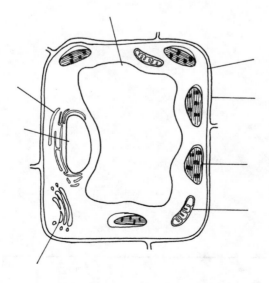

Activity: Create a poster that lists the three main points of the cell theory. Illustrate it with a detailed and colorful drawing of an animal or plant cell.

Chapter 10 Review

1) Define matter and list the three forms of matter.

2) Give two examples of elements and their symbols from the Periodic Table of Elements.

3) Compare a compound with a mixture.

4) What is a molecule?

5) Cells are the basic _____ of life.

6) All cells contain what three parts?

7) Compare a prokaryotic and eukaryotic cell.

8) Name one important scientist in the forming of the cell theory and describe his important accomplishment.

9) How are new cells formed?

10) Match these organelles with the function they perform:

A.   endoplasmic reticulum
B.   vacuoles
C.   lysosomes
D.   golgi bodies
E.   chloroplasts
F.   mitochondria
G.   cell membrane
H.   nucleus
I.   chloroplasts
J.   cytoplasm

1. _____ The gel-like material inside the cell membrane that carries out the life processes of the cell

2. _____ The organelles in plant cells that make food by changing light energy into chemical energy

3. _____ The janitors of the cell contain chemicals that digest wastes, worn-out cell parts, and food

4. _____ The flexible, outer structure of a cell that gives it shape and regulates what enters and leaves the cell.

5. _____ The cell's brain. It directs the activities of the cell.

6. _____ The conveyer belt for the cell. It moves materials around the cell

7. _____ The rigid structure outside the cell membrane that supports and protects the plant cell

8. _____ The powerhouse of the cell. It supplies energy for the cell

9. _____ The packaging plant and loading dock for proteins

10. _____ The warehouses of the cell. They store water, food, and waste products

Student Objectives
Chapter 11: Minerals, Rocks ,and Soil

My objectives are:

1) Using the Mohs hardness scale, I will compare the hardness of several minerals.

2) Using information about the rock cycle, I will find a rock and hypothesize about its type and history.

3) I will label a diagram of the three different horizons of mature soil.

4) I will observe a topsoil sample and list the types of soil particles and organic matter in my sample.

5) I will list three factors that help soil develop.

Chapter 11: Minerals, Rocks ,and Soil

O Lord, how manifold are Your works! In wisdom You have made them all. The earth is full of Your possessions.

Psalm 104:24

The natural world is a wonderful creation. Exploring the natural world with all of your senses shows what a diverse and interesting piece of work the world is. Everything that you physically experience was made by God. Truly, the earth is full of God's possessions — minerals, metals, rocks, precious gems, and other interesting things that come from the earth's storehouses.

In this chapter, we will study minerals, rocks and soil. Minerals are what form rocks, and rocks are broken up into soil. Many minerals of the earth are considered to be very useful and precious to us. God, who created each mineral, also considers minerals to be precious. In the Old Testament, God often gave specific instructions on how priestly garments and the temple were to be decorated with rare and beautiful treasures. However, God also warned against putting too much emphasis on obtaining these treasures. He is more concerned with the state of our hearts than with the riches we own.

We use rocks in many ways, but especially in building. Throughout the Bible, rocks are referred to as strong foundations upon which we should build. We are told to build our house upon the rock (Christ), rather than on sinking sand. Jesus is considered to be the cornerstone of the church. Christ also called Peter the rock upon which He would build the Church. Look around your neighborhood and see how rocks are used.

Soil is also used as a practical illustration for our lives. In Matthew, Jesus relates different kinds of soil to the readiness of our hearts. Because many of the people to whom Jesus spoke were simple farmers, his parables often discussed soil and its many aspects. Learning more about the scientific side of minerals, rocks, and soil should enhance and enrich our understanding of the Bible. Read on and enjoy the new meanings you will find as a result!

Section 11-1: Minerals

We will now travel to a display case at the Smithsonian Institution in Washington, D.C., where the Hope Diamond now rests. The Hope Diamond is a large, dark-blue gem with a dramatic history. The diamond was owned and worn by King Louis XVI of France, who was later beheaded during the French Revolution. The Diamond disappeared after the revolution, and reappeared nearly forty years later. As it passed from owner to owner in Europe and the United States, it was linked with murders, tragic accidents, and other misfortunes.

The Hope iamond is an example of a mineral. The definition of a **mineral** is a naturally occurring, inorganic solid with a definite crystal structure and chemical composition. Five important characteristics are listed in this definition, and all must be met in order for a substance to be classified as a mineral. Let's look at these characteristics more closely.

NATURALLY OCCURRING: A mineral must occur naturally in the Earth. Steel and cement are manufactured materials, so they are not considered minerals.

INORGANIC: Inorganic means that the minerals are not alive, never were alive, and are not made by life processes. Coal and oil meet the first characteristic of naturally occurring underground. However, since they are formed from the remains of living things, they are not considered minerals.

SOLID: A solid has a definite volume and shape. A gas such as oxygen is naturally occurring and inorganic. However, it has no shape. A liquid such as water also occurs naturally and is inorganic, yet it has no shape. These things are not considered minerals.

CRYSTAL STRUCTURE: A crystal is a solid in which the atoms are arranged in a pattern that is repeated over and over again. A crystal has flat sides that meet in sharp edges and corners. For example, the atoms contained in each grain of salt form a cube. Because this is repeated, it is considered a mineral. However an opal would not be considered a mineral because its atoms are not arranged in a definite structure.

CHEMICAL COMPOSITION: Every mineral is an element or compound with a chemical composition that is unique to that mineral.

Scientists have discovered about 2500 different kinds of minerals. This wide variety of minerals can make it very difficult to tell them apart. However, each mineral possesses certain physical properties that are used to identify it. Learning about these properties can help us to identify a mineral. Let's learn about these properties.

HARDNESS: A measure of how easily a mineral can be scratched is its hardness. Friedrich Mohs, a German mineralogist, used ten minerals and arranged them in order of increasing hardness. The Mohs scale assigns the number 1 to the softest mineral, talc, and the number 10, to the hardest mineral, diamond. Each mineral will scratch any mineral with a lower number. Look at the Mohs hardness scale on the following page and answer the questions.

Mineral	Hard	Home Tests
Talc	1	Easily scratched by fingernail
Gypsum	2	Scratched by fingernail
Calcite	3	Very easily scratched with knife
Fluorite	4	Easily scratched with knife
Apatite	5	Difficult to scratch with knife
Feldspars	6	Scratched with steel knife/may scratch glass
Quartz	7	Scratches steel file/scratches glass easily
Topaz	8	Scratches steel file/scratches glass easily
Corundum	9	Scratches steel file/scratches glass easily
Diamond	10	Scratches steel file/scratches glass easily

1. Name a mineral which is harder than talc, but softer than quartz?

2. What minerals can corundum, the mineral from which rubies and sapphires are made, scratch?

3. Would gypsum be considered a soft or hard mineral?

COLOR: Color helps to identify a mineral, but cannot be used alone. For example, the saying "all that glitters is not gold" is true. Two other minerals, chalcopyrite and pyrite (fool's gold) are minerals with the same color, but are not gold. There are a few minerals that always have the same color. Sulfur has a distinctive yellow color. Malachite is always green, and azurite is always

307

blue. However, many other minerals come in a variety of colors or their color changes as a result of exposure. Color must be used with other tests to positively identify a mineral.

LUSTER: Luster describes how light is reflected from a mineral's surface. Luster is defined as either metallic or nonmetallic. Minerals that do not reflect much light have a nonmetallic luster. Minerals that reflect light the way highly polished metal does have a metallic luster.

STREAK: The color of the mineral when it is broken up and powdered is called its streak. Many minerals can be tested by rubbing the mineral across a piece of unglazed porcelain tile, or streak plate. Though the color of a mineral may vary, its streak is always the same. Gold can be identified by a yellow streak, whereas pyrite, or fool's gold, has a greenish black or brown-black streak. Minerals that are harder than the streak plate cannot be identified this way because they only scratch the tile, rather than crumble into powder. Also, minerals with a white or colorless streak, such as talc, gypsum, and quartz, are difficult to identify by using this test only.

CLEAVAGE AND FRACTURE: The way a mineral breaks is another clue to its identity. Minerals that break along smooth, flat surfaces have cleavage. Minerals that break with rough or jagged edges have fracture.

OTHER PROPERTIES: Other minerals have special properties that help identify them. Fluorite glows when put under ultraviolet light. Magnetite is attracted by magnets. Sulfur smells like rotten eggs. These unusual characteristics help to differentiate one mineral from another.

Section 11-2: Rocks

Many people have a hobby of collecting unique rocks. Wherever they go in the outdoors, they look for a special find that they can take home and add to their collection. It is a popular hobby because rocks are everywhere, and yet, each rock is unique.

What is a rock? A rock is a hard substance that is usually made up of two or more minerals mixed together. For example, granite is a mixture of feldspar, quartz, mica, hornblende, and other minerals.

How do rocks form? We learned how the earth's crust is formed by three types of rock: sedimentary, igneous, and metamorphic. These three types of rock are always changing from one form or another in a process called the rock cycle. All rocks are formed by and are a part of the rock cycle, including those used to build houses, buildings, and monuments. Let's learn more about this process.

IGNEOUS: Though the rock cycle is continuous, we will begin exploring it by visiting the depths of the earth between 60 and 200 kilometers. The rocks at this depth are under great pressure and generate thermal energy which heats them.

The heat and pressure in some parts of the earth eventually melt the rocks to form magma. As we learned in the chapter on volcanoes, magma is forced to the surface where it becomes lava. When lava cools, it hardens to form igneous rocks.

METAMORPHIC: Sometimes there is not enough heat or pressure to melt the rocks found at the depths we just discussed. In areas where melting doesn't occur, some of the substances are flattened. Sometimes minerals exchange atoms with surrounding minerals, and new or bigger minerals form. Depending upon the amount of pressure applied, one type of rock can change into several different metamorphic rocks.

SEDIMENTARY: Weathering is a process that breaks rocks into smaller pieces. Rocks are broken down and then moved in a process called erosion. Sediments come from already-existing rocks that are weathered and eroded. If sediments are small, the pressure of layers and layers of sediments deposited by erosion will cause compaction. If sediments are large, pressure must be accompanied by water, which dissolves minerals that help to cement the sediments together. This process is called cementation. These two processes help to form sedimentary rocks.

All these rocks are changing their forms all the time. Look at the diagram below. Notice that each type of rock can form another type under the right circumstances.

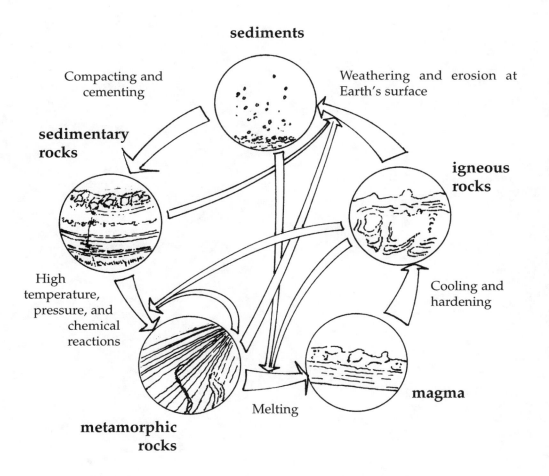

Activity: Find a rock and make a guess what type it is. Using the information you just read about the rock cycle, write a story about its history. How did it arrive in this place? How did it get its form, its size, its composition, and its color?

_____

_____

_____

_____

_____

_____

_____

_____

Section 11-3: Soil

In the previous section, we discussed weathering, the process that breaks down rock into smaller pieces. When rocks are continuously broken down by weathering, soil is formed. What is soil? **Soil** is a mixture of weathered rock, organic matter, mineral fragments, water, and air. Soil is what supports vegetation by providing plants with minerals and water needed for growth. Animals also depend on soil indirectly. Some animals eat plants. Other animals eat animals that eat plants. It is easy to see that soil is an important part of our survival on Earth.

Soil is a mixture of substances, but the two main ingredients of soil are pieces of weathered rock and organic material. Beneath soil is a layer of rock called **bedrock.** This bedrock is constantly undergoing the weathering process to make soil. Sometimes the soil remains above the bedrock from which it was formed. This type of soil is called **residual soil.** Some soil is moved away by water, wind, glaciers, and waves. This type of soil is called **transported soil.**

Organic material is produced by the decay of plants and animals. This decaying, organic material is called **humus.** Humus is dark-colored, and is important for the growth of plants. Humus also helps to further break down the rocks which help to make soil. Look at the diagram on the following page.

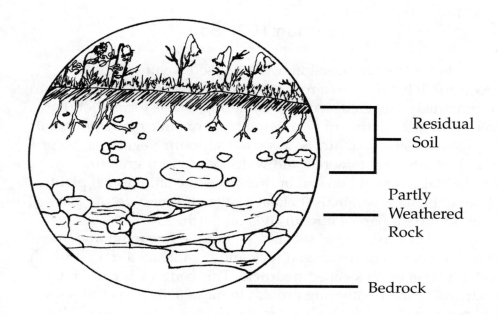

Residual
Soil

Partly
Weathered
Rock

Bedrock

SOIL HORIZONS: As soil forms, it develops separate soil layers
called horizons. Each soil horizon is different. If the soil has
developed recently, it probably has only two layers and is called
immature soil. With the proper conditions and much time, three
layers can develop into what is called mature soil. We will look at
the three layers of mature soil.

The top layer of mature soil is called the A horizon. The
soil in the A horizon is called **topsoil.** It is a dark-colored soil
layer in which much activity by living organisms takes place.
Topsoil consists mostly of humus and other organic materials. It
stores water well, and allows both air and water to reach the roots

of plants. Topsoil is the most fertile part of the soil.

Both immature and mature soils contain the B and C horizons. The B horizon is just below the A horizon. It is called **subsoil.** Subsoil is formed very slowly. It is made of clay, humus, and, in mature soil, some minerals that have been washed down from the topsoil. The C horizon consists of partly weathered rock. It extends down to the top of the bedrock, and its composition is very similar to the bedrock. Look at the diagram of mature soil below and label its three different horizons with these words: *topsoil, subsoil,* and *partly weathered rock.*

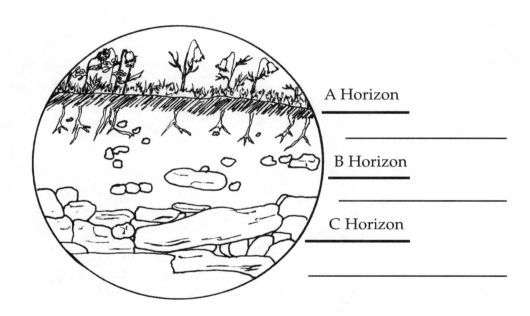

A Horizon
_____

_____

B Horizon
_____

_____

C Horizon
_____

_____

Activity: Examining topsoil

Materials: magnifying glass and a topsoil sample

1. Obtain a topsoil sample from a garden center, or a forest or grassy area.

2. Using the magnifying glass, separate the small particles of soil from the particles of organic material.

What types of soil particles and organic matter are in your sample?

HOW DOES SOIL DEVELOP? — What are the factors that help mature soil to develop? One of the most important factors is time. The longer a rock is exposed to the forces of weathering, the more it is broken down. Climate is another factor. Areas with heavy rainfall and warm temperatures help to weather the soil more quickly. The type of rock in an area also is a factor in soil development. Rocks that do not break down easily do not form soil rapidly. Some rocks, such as sandstone, break and crumble easily and form soil quickly. The slope of a region also determines how easily soil will develop. On very steep slopes, rainwater does not have a chance to sink into the soil and weather the rocks below. In the lines provided, list three factors that help soil development.

1. _____

_____

2. _____

_____

3. _____

_____

Chapter 11 Review

1) What are the five characteristics of a mineral?

2) Name three ways a mineral can be identified and explain them.

3) What is a rock?

4) Define weathering, erosion, compaction, and cementation.

5) Soil is made mainly of what two ingredients?

6) Compare residual soil with transported soil.

7) Compare topsoil with subsoil.

Chapter 11: Plants
Student Objectives

My objectives are:

1) I will create a concept map of the different groups and divisions of plants.

2) I will draw an example of a gymnosperm and an angiosperm.

3) I will label the major parts of a leaf.

4) I will complete an illustration of the gymnosperm reproductive cycle.

5) I will match important terms with appropriate definitions in a diagram of an angiosperm seed.

6) I will dissect a seed and list its major parts.

Chapter 12: Plants

"He causes the grass to grow for the cattle, vegetation for the service of man, That he may bring forth food from the earth; And wine that makes glad the heart of man, Oil to make his face shine, And bread which strengthens man's heart, The trees of the Lord are full of sap; the cedars of Lebanon, which He planted."

Psalm 104: 14-16

God's original home for His special creation, man, was a garden. The Garden of Eden must have been a beautiful place with bowers of flowers, groves of various fruit trees, and the most delectable vegetables. His design was both functional and pleasurable. "The Lord God planted a garden ... the Lord God made every tree grow that is pleasant to the sight and good for food," Genesis 2:9.

Though we have come a long way from the Garden of Eden, God's creation is still both functional and beautiful. Plants are an important part of our diet. They beautify our surroundings, whether they are indoors or outdoors. They serve as the basis for many medicines that help to cure ailments or lessen pain. They also cleanse the air we breathe.

Plants are one of those "good gifts" to God's children. As we learn about the diversity of plants, think about the creativity God used to create each kind. As the verse in Psalms says, He designed plants to serve us, help us, strengthen us, and make us glad. Our proper response should be praise!

We will first visit the land of the giants. When we read about Jack and the Beanstalk, giants seem to be loud, bumbling, gigantic people. However, in this land, the giants are serene, wise, old and venerable. They are regal, arranging themselves like nobility in a royal hall in medieval times. The hall is quiet. Only soft sounds are made, just a little louder than whispering. The hall

is beautifully decorated with greenery. Lovely courtyards are
interspered in the palace design. We are walking through the red-
wood forests of California.

Section 12-1: Division of Plants

Plants are a diverse group of living things. About 285,000 plant species have been identified, and scientists believe that there are more still to be found. They range in size from giant sequoia trees which are 100 meters in height, to tiny water ferns that are so small they require a magnifying glass to see. Plants are also highly adaptable. They are found in ice-covered Antarctica and in the hot, dry deserts of Africa.

However, there are certain characteristics that all plants have in common. All plants are made of many eukaryotic cells. Cell walls surround plant cells and provide structure. Most plants contain the green pigment called chlorophyll. Chlorophyll is formed by chloroplasts. In the chapter that discussed cells, we learned that chloroplasts are organelles specific to plants. They change light energy into chemical energy. In other words, they convert sunlight into food. Most plants have roots or rootlike structures that hold them in the ground. Thus, most plants do not move around. Most plants live on land, but many live in or near water.

Plants are classified into major groups called divisions. Look at the diagram of plant divisions on the next page. All of these plant groups are related, but have differences that are suffi-cient to separate them from other groups. These divisions are grouped together into two categories: simple plants and complex plants. Simple plants are seedless plants; complex plants are seed plants. Let's learn about these two categories.

Write "plants" in the top circle of the concept map below. In the left box branching from the top circle, write "seedless," and in the circle to the right of it, write "seed."

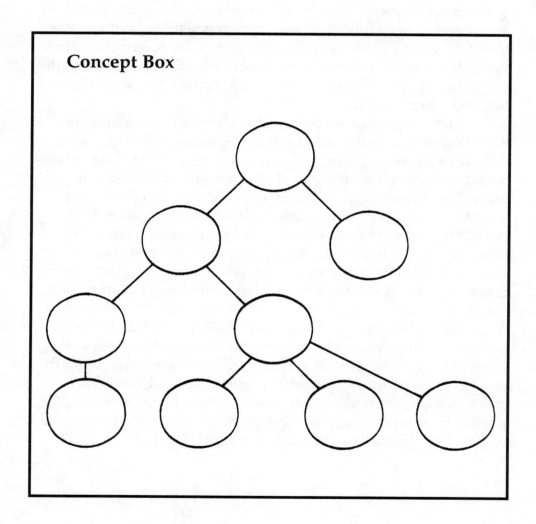

Concept Box

Section 12-2: Seedless Plants

Seedless plants are simple plants that grow from spores rather than seeds. There are two types of seedless plants: nonvascular and vascular. Vascular plants are able to grow taller than nonvascular plants because they contain tissue that can transport nutrients up through the plant.

SEEDLESS, NON-VASCULAR PLANTS: Seedless, nonvascular plants have none of the parts that one would usually associate with plants. These simple plants have rootlike fibers, but not roots; stalks that look like stems, but not stems; and leaflike green growths, but not leaves. Seedless, non-vascular plants called **bryophytes.**Mosses and liverworts are included in this category.

Mosses and liverworts: Mosses and liverworts are simple, small plants found in damp environments. They are without vascular tissue, and thus, grow very close to the ground. Because they are just a few cells thick, they are able to absorb water directly through their cell walls.

SEEDLESS, VASCULAR PLANTS: These plants are simple, but differ from mosses because they have vascular tissue. Vascular tissue is made up of long, tubelike cells in which water and nutrients are transported through the plant. Plants with vascular tissue are able to grow taller than seedless, non-vascular plants because they can transport nutrients to their upper parts. However, seedless vascular plants do not reach more than one or two meters in height. This group includes the divisions of club mosses and spike mosses, horsetails, and ferns.

Club mosses and spike mosses: Club mosses and spike mosses produce spores at the end of stems in structures similar to pine cones. The upright stems of club mosses have needlelike leaves. Spike mosses look very similar to club mosses.

Horsetails and ferns have a jointed stems, and a hollow centers surrounded by a ring of vascular tissue. Leaves grow in a spiral around each joint. Spores grow at the tip of the stem. Most ferns produce spores in special structures on the leaves. Ferns are the largest group of seedless, vascular plants.

Activity: Turn back to the concept map on page 328. Write "vascular" and "nonvascular" in the two boxes branching from the word "seedless." List the divisions of these two types in the remaining boxes.

Section 12-3: Seed Plants

Nearly all the plants you are familiar with are seed plants. Seed plants have roots, stems, leaves, and vascular tissue. A seed plant differs from a simple plant in that it grows from a seed. Seed plants are divided into two major groups: gymnosperms and angiosperms.

GYMNOSPERMS: Gymnosperms are vascular plants that produce seeds on the scales of female cones. The name gymnosperm means "naked seed." Seeds of gymnosperms are not protected by fruit. Gymnosperms do not produce flowers. Most gymnosperms produce leaves that are needlelike or scalelike and keep their leaves for several years. This group includes the divisions of conifers, ginkgos, cycads, and gnetums.

Conifers: This division includes the pines, firs, spruces, cedars, and junipers. You are probably most familiar with this division. Most of the wood used for building construction and for paper production comes from conifers such as pines and spruces. The waxy substance secreted by conifers is used to make chemicals found in soap, paint, varnish, and some medicines. The conifer division produces the greatest number of species of gymnosperms.

Ginkgos: Today, the ginkoes are represented by only one living species. It is a tree, so it has a large, richly branched stem, and smaller, simple leaves.

Cycads: About 100 species of cycads exist today. These plants have small sparsely branched stems and large, compound leaves.

Gnetums: Most living gnetophytes can be found in the deserts or mountains of Asia, Africa, and Central or South America. Most of these plants are vinelike, woody plants with broad leaves.

ANGIOSPERMS: Angiosperms are a division of their own. These plants are vascular plants in which the seed is enclosed inside a fruit. A fruit is a ripened part of the plant that produces seeds. All angiosperms produce flowers. More than half of all known plant species are angiosperms.

The importance of angiosperms is that they form the basis for the diets of most animals. For humans, angiosperms produce fruits and vegetables, legumes such as peas and lentils, and the grains we use in bread. They also produce the fibers we use in our clothing, such as flax and cotton.

Activity: In the spaces below, draw an example of a gymnosperm and an angiosperm. Remember, gymnosperms usually have pine cones, and angiosperms have flowers and fruits.

Angiosperm

Gymnosperm

Section 12-4: Parts of Complex Plants

All seed plants have three common structures: leaves, stems, and roots. Let's learn about the basics of complex plants.

LEAVES: Leaves are designed to help plants survive on land by conserving water. The **epidermis** acts as a protective layer that covers both the upper and lower surfaces of a leaf. The **cuticle** is a waxy substance that protects the plant from wilting or drying out. **Stomata** are small pores in the leaf that allow carbon dioxide, water, and oxygen to enter and leave the leaf. The stomata are surrounded by **guard cells** that open and close the pores.

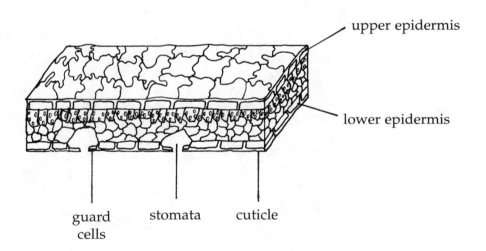

upper epidermis

lower epidermis

guard
cells

stomata

cuticle

STEMS: Stems are the parts of plants that support leaves and flowers. The stem's main function is to support the plant and to move materials between the leaves and roots. Stems can look very different from plant to plant. The trunk of a tree is its stem. Potatoes and onions are underground stems with stored food.

ROOTS: The root system of most plants is as large or larger than the above-ground stems and leaves. This is where water and minerals enter the plant. The vascular tissue of plants moves water and minerals from the roots up through the stem and out to the leaves. Roots also anchor plants in soil, and store food. When you eat carrots or beets, you are actually eating the roots made of stored food.

Section 12-5: Complex Plant Reproduction

What is reproduction? **Reproduction** is the process by which plants and animals create offspring. Simple plants reproduce from spores. Complex plants reproduce from seeds. A seed is designed to survive unfavorable environmental conditions. A seed has parts that store food and cause the plant to grow when conditions are favorable.

Gymnosperm Fertilization

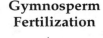

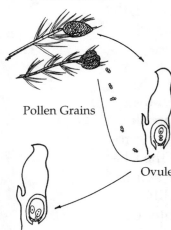

Pollen Grains

Ovule

Pollen Tube

In gymnosperms, seeds usually form on cones. In angiosperms, seeds are formed in the fruit of the plant. Let's learn about the different ways gymnosperms and angiosperms reproduce.

GYMNOSPERM REPRODUCTION: In studying how gymnosperms reproduce, we will use a pine tree as an example. Each pine tree produces male and female cones. Male cones are smaller than female cones, and produce pollen grains which contain the sperm. Wind carries the pollen grain to the female gymnosperm cones.

A female cone has a spiral of woody scales on a short stem. Two ovules are produced on top of each scale. (Ovules are the female reproductive part of the plant.) Inside the ovule is an egg cell. On the outside of the ovule is a sticky fluid. The sticky fluid serves to catch the pollen grains given off by the male cone.

When pollen grains land on an ovule, a pollen tube grows from the pollen grain to the ovule. A sperm swims down the pollen tube and fertilizes the egg cell in a process called **pollination.** A seed develops as a result. The female cone will then release its seeds during the fall or winter months. The seeds are carried away, eaten, or buried by animals. The buried seeds will eventually grow into a plant when the right conditions are present.

Using the text and the diagram on the following page, fill in the blanks with the correct word.

337

1. Male cones produce _____.

2. Wind carries pollen grains to _____.

3. Pollen grains land on an _____.

4. A pollen tube grows from the _____ to the _____.

5. A sperm moves down the pollen tube and _____ the egg cell.

6. A _____ develops.

ANGIOSPERM REPRODUCTION: Flowers contain the reproductive organs of angiosperms. Inside each flower are the male reproductive organ called the **stamen,** and the female reproductive organ called the **pistil.** The sperm of the stamen reaches the pistil in different ways. In large, brightly colored flowers, insects and other animals pollinate the flower while feeding on the flower's nectar and pollen. Flowers that aren't brightly colored often depend on wind for pollination. Their petals may be small, or the flowers may have no petals at all. The flowers of wheat are an example. Once the flower is

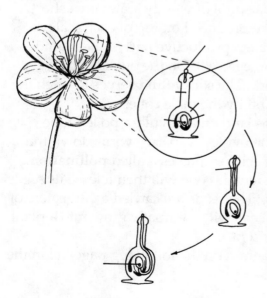

pollinated, the sperm travels down the pollen tube and fertilizes the egg. A seed then develops.

The seeds of an angiosperm travel from the flower to the ground in a variety of ways. Some are dispersed by the wind. Others are scattered by becoming attached to the fur or feathers of animals. Some float on water. Once a seed reaches the ground, it will stay there until the right conditions occur for the plant to grow.

How does a seed develop? A seed is covered in a protective layer called the seed coat. Inside the seed is the embryo. The embryo is a fertilized egg that will eventually grow into a plant. Inside the embryo, both the stem and root are present. Outside the embryo are the cotyledons. The cotyledons store food for the embryo plant. When conditions are favorable, the plant will begin to grow outside of the seed.

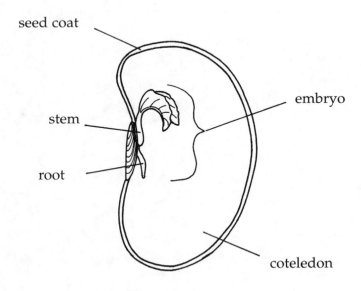

Activity: Obtain a lima bean or other large seed and dissect it to find out what is inside. If the seed is hard and dry, place it in water overnight. Carefully pull apart the halves of the seed and look for the parts of the embryo plant on one side of the seed. Write down your observations.

Chapter 12 Review

1. Compare seedless plants with seed plants.

2. What is the function of a plant's vascular tissue?

3. Name three divisions of simple (seedless) plants.

4. Compare gymnosperms with angiosperms.

5. What are some ways we use conifers?

6. What is a fruit?

7. How do we use angiosperms?

8. List and describe the three parts common to complex plants.

9. Define reproduction.

10. What is the function of a seed?

11. Fertilization in plants is called _____.

12. Name two ways pollination occurs in angiosperms.

Student Objectives
Chapter 13: Animals

My objectives are:

1. I will define the word "animal" using the five characteristics of animals.

2. I will create a poster of the five characteristics of animals and illustrate it.

3. I will draw an imaginary animal, classify it, and list its defining characteristics.

4. I will demonstrate how filter feeders eat in an experiment.

5. I will identify the different characteristics of arthropods in a chart.

6. I will identify invertebrates in the wild and categorize them into phyla.

7. I will list the major stages of the frog's metamorphosis.

8. I will describe a pet by listing its defining characteristics.

9. I will compare these words: organism, population, community, ecosystem, and biosphere.

10. I will list three producers and three consumers in a food web.

Chapter 13: Animals

"And God said, 'Let the water teem with living creatures, and let birds fly above the earth across the expanse of the sky.' So God created the great creatures of the sea and every living and moving thing with which the water teems, according to their kinds, and every winged bird according to its kind...

And God said, 'Let the land produce living creatures according to their kinds: livestock, creatures that move along the ground, and wild animals, each according to its kind.' And it was so. God made the wild animals according to their kinds, the livestock according to their kinds, and all the creatures that move along the ground according to their kinds. And God saw that it was good."

Genesis 1:20-26

There are phrases in this passage that indicate to any reader the vastness of God's creativity. Phrases such as "Let the water teem..." and "across the expanse of the sky" help the reader to understand that God did not make just a few starter water creatures that eventually evolved into all the animals that we see today.

However, there are other phrases that speak directly to the scientist. Phrases such as "every living and moving thing" (in water) and "all the creatures that move along the ground" may be skimmed over by the non-scientist. A scientist, however, would recognize just how many living things there are. The animals we see and know, the larger animals with fur or hair, four legs, and a tail, are only a tiny part of the gigantic kingdom of animals. Did you know that 97 percent of all animal species are invertebrates — the types of animals that <u>don't</u> have fur or hair, four legs, and a tail? Did you know that there are more than 700,000 classified species of insects, and scientists describe more each year?

The writer of Genesis probably had very little knowledge

about this massive part of the animal kingdom. However, it is interesting to note that the writing somehow includes this unseen part. God knew about the diversity of His creation. He knew that one day we would begin to explore it. The fascinating part about it is that we never exhausted and will never exhaust the subject. There will always be more species to find. There will always be more to study about any one animal. God has provided enough discovery in this world to last us an eternity. We humans will forever be saying, "Aha! So that is how God does that!"

Section 13-1: Characteristics of Animals

In the introduction, we discussed how vast and diverse the animal kingdom is. The animal kingdom includes the fly, the elephant, the wor,m and the whale. However, for all the millions of species to be considered animals, they must have some common characteristics. What are those characteristics?

1. Animals have many cells. However, just because something has many cells does not make it an animal. Plants have many cells as well.

2. Animal cells are eukaryotic. Again, plants also have cells that are eukaryotic. Remember that eukaryotic cells have a nucleus and organelles surrounded by membranes. Eukaryotic cells are the more complex cells that carry out multiple functions such as reproduction, digestion, and getting rid of wastes.

3. Animals cannot make their own food. This is where animals and plants differ. Plants can make their own food using the sun's energy. Animals, however, depend on other living things for food. Some animals eat plants. Some animals eat other animals. Some animals, like humans, eat both plants and other animals.

4. Animals digest their food. This is another difference from plants. Plants do not digest food; they produce food. Digestion is the process of breaking down food into substances the body can absorb.

5. Most animals are mobile. Remember that most plants are stationary? They are rooted in the ground and stay in one place. Since animals must depend on other living things in order to survive, they must be able to move to find the plants or animals they need to eat.

Using these five characteristics, write a definition of an animal on the lines below.

_____

_____

_____

_____

Activity: Create a poster titled "What is an animal?" Write down the characteristics of animals and illustrate it with cut-out pictures of animals from magazines.

Section 13-2: Classifying Animals

Scientists have divided the kingdom of animals into nine different groups called phyla. However, before we discuss each phyla, it is important to know how scientists divide animals into groups. The first characteristic a scientist looks for is whether the animal has a backbone. If an animal does not have a backbone, the animal is classified as an **invertebrate.** About 97 percent of all animal species are invertebrates. If the animal does have a backbone, the animal is called a **vertebrate.** These are the more recognizable animals to us — fish, reptiles, birds and mammals. These are a few examples of vertebrates.

The next characteristic a scientist looks for is symmetry. **Symmetry** is the way an animal's body parts are arranged. Very simple animals that have no definite shape have **asymmetry.** Animals that have body parts arranged around a central point, like spokes are arranged on a bicycle wheel, have **radial symmetry.** Most animals have **bilateral symmetry.** This means that if an imaginary line were drawn down the middle of an animal, the two sides would mirror each other. Its body parts are arranged the same way on both sides. Humans have bilateral symmetry. Our bodies look the same on both sides. Look at the diagram on the following page.

Once the animal is categorized as an invertebrate or vertebrate, and the symmetry of the animal has been decided, a scientist will begin to identify characteristics it has in common with other animals. Perhaps the animal stings its prey before eating it. Perhaps it has a hard shell. Perhaps it lives in water. The animal may lay eggs, or provide milk for its young. We will learn more about these different characteristics in the next sections.

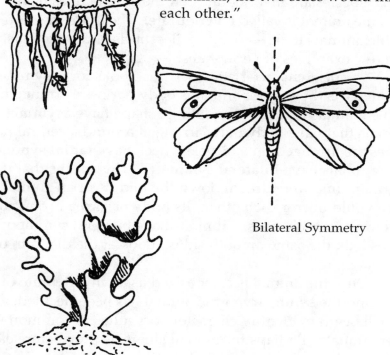

Radial Symmetry

"**Symmetry** is the way an animal's body parts are arranged. Very simple animals that have no definite shape have **asymmetry.** Animals that have body parts arranged around a central point, like spokes are arranged on a bicycle wheel, have **radial symmetry.** Most animals have **bilateral symmetry.** This means that, if an imaginary line were drawn down the middle of an animal, the two sides would mirror each other."

Bilateral Symmetry

Asymmetry

350

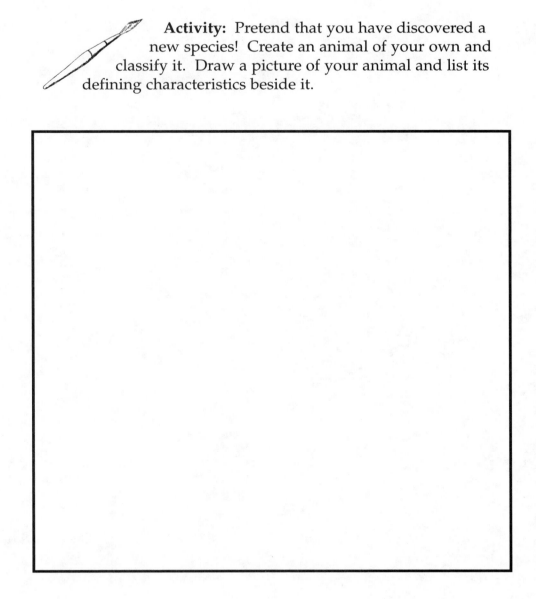

Activity: Pretend that you have discovered a new species! Create an animal of your own and classify it. Draw a picture of your animal and list its defining characteristics beside it.

Section 13-3: Invertebrates

Recall that invertebrates are animals without a backbone. This group of animals makes up most of the animal kingdom in numbers.   However, these animals tend to go unnoticed, perhaps because many are small in size, found in rare places, live in water or should be avoided. There is extreme diversity among this group, as you will see. Enjoy yourself as you explore this "invisible" part of the animal world.

We will make a visit to the ocean floor. Rather than travel to the ocean's depths, we will go to the warm, shallow, salt water near the coast. As we look around us, there are many beautiful and colorful creatures to see. However, the organism for which we are looking will not swim past us. Instead, we are looking for an organism that is rooted in the ground. Now, we see it. It has long tubes that are taller than we are. In fact, it is larger than a compact car. It is a soft purple color. As we draw closer, we can see the many pores, and the neon green algae that grows on it. It does not have any definite shape. There are no eyes, ears, or mouth. In fact, it looks like an exotic plant of some sort. Yet, it is an animal. What is it? Keep reading and find out.

SPONGE: The sponge is one of the least complex animals in body structure in the animal kingdom, along with the cnidarians, flatworms, and roundworms. Years ago, scientists believed sponges to be plants because they have simple body plans and no body tissues, organs, or organ systems. All sponges live in water. They grow in many shapes, sizes, and colors. Most do not have any definite shape (asymmetrical). They also live attached to one place, once they have matured. So what makes these plant-like organisms animals? Once scientists observed that sponges could not make their own food, they classified them as animals. Sponges eat bacteria, algae, protozoans, and other materials by filtering them out of the water. That is why sponges are called **filter feeders.**

Activity: How does the sponge eat?
Materials: bath sponge, scissors, two glasses, coffee grounds or coarse, ground pepper

1) Cut the bath sponge so that it is about one to two inches bigger than the bottom of the glass.

2) Put the sponge half way down inside the glass, leaving at least one to two inches at the top and the bottom.

3) Mix one cup of water with one tablespoon of coffee grounds or coarse, ground pepper.

4) Pour the mixture over the sponge.

5) Write your observations and conclusions in a paragraph. Answer these questions: What was the difference between the water in the bottom of the glass and the water you poured? How does this experiment relate to how sponges filter feed?

Now we will rise to just under the surface of the ocean. Surrounding us is a beautiful coral reef. Many exotic looking creatures swim in and out of the reef. As we look up, we see what looks like an alien life form. It has a circular, mushroom top that is almost transparent. An orange tint colors the liquid inside the organism. Hanging from this structure are long, blood-red strands. Some of them are over 15 meters long. Amidst these strands hangs a pink, cloudy substance that is attached to the organism's underside. A large fish swims by and barely touches the alien. It stops in the water. Slowly the alien uses its tentacles to pull the organism into the cloudy substance and then absorbs it. What is this alien?

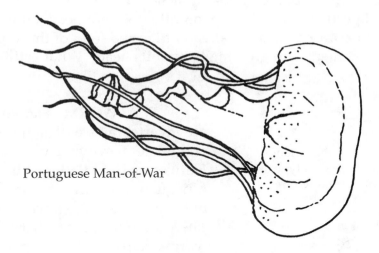

Portuguese Man-of-War

CNIDARIAN: The creature we just saw was a Portuguese man-of-war. It is an example of a cnidarian. The word "cnidaria" is Latin for "stinging cells." All members of this phyla contain stinging cells. The stinging cell is a capsule that contains a coiled harpoon-like thread and poison. When a small organism bumps

355

into the "trigger," the capsule explodes and shoots out its thread and poison, paralyzing the organism. Then the cnidarian wraps its tentacles around the victim and pulls it into the mouth. Some examples of cnidarians are the sea anemone, the coral, and the Portuguese man-of-war.

To see the next organism, we will have to shrink ourselves to fit inside another animal. As we travel into this animal's intestines, we see it. This organism is attached to the intestinal tissue of the animal in which we are traveling. It is extremely long, thin, pink, flat, and has many segments. The body looks like a pink ribbon hanging from the intestine. Its head looks like a suction cup with many barbed hooks attached to it. There is no mouth or digestive system. It apparently does not need a digestive system because it eats the already digested food of the animal. New body segments are growing behind its head. What is this creature?

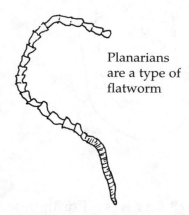

Planarians are a type of flatworm

FLATWORM: Flatworms are invertebrates with soft bodies and bilateral symmetry. Flatworms have flattened bodies. Most flatworms live in salt water, but some live in fresh water. There are two types of flatworms: tapeworms and planarians. Tapeworms are parasites. A **parasite** is an animal that depends on another animal for food and a place to live. The animal on which the parasite depends is called its **host**. When a parasite is attached to its host, it benefits the parasite, but harms the host. Tapeworms use hooks and suckers to attach themselves to the intestine of its host. Dogs,

356

cats, humans, and other animals are hosts for tapeworms.

Tapeworms are parasitic
flatworms.

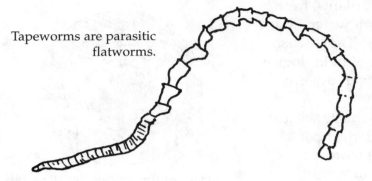

Planarians are **free-living.** Free-living organisms do not
depend on one particular organism for food or a place to live. A
planarian feeds on small organisms and dead bodies of larger
organisms. The planarian has a triangle-shaped head with two
eyespots. The body is covered with **cilia,** which are tiny hair-like
structures that help the worm to move.

Now, we will visit the home of another parasite. We will
continue to travel as a tiny, microscopic ship, because the creature
we want to see is also microscopic. This one is waiting in the soil
for a host to walk by. This is also an elongated organism, though
not as long as the tapeworm. It is slender and tapered at both
ends. Unlike the organisms that we have visited so far, this one
has two body openings, one at each end. It turns to look at us.
The eyeless monster has a round head. Its mouth is a jagged
opening.

ROUNDWORM: Roundworms are slender and tapered at
both ends. Unlike the organisms we have studied so far, roundworms have a mouth and an anus. The **anus** is an opening at the
end of the digestive tract where wastes leave the body. More than
a half million species of roundworms are estimated to exist.

Roundworms are found in soil, animals, plants, fresh water, and salt water. Many are parasites. The disease called heartworm in dogs is caused by a roundworm parasite.

Hookworms are very small round-worms. Magnification: 200X

The parasite we just visited is called a hook-worm. Hookworms are parasites of humans. Humans get hookworm by walking barefoot over dirt or through fields.

Now we will enlarge ourselves to our regular size and return to the ocean. As we dive into the ocean and aim for the ocean floor, we disturb a group of organisms which are surrounded by two shells hooked together with a hinge. These animals begin to "clap" their shells and in the process move themselves quickly to a distant rock. It almost looks as if they are applauding our arrival!

We look out the other window of our ship and see an animal that is familiar to us all. It has eight arms with suction cups on the underside of each arm. Two large eyes bulge from the domed head. Our movement disturbs the creature, and a jet of water shoots from its head, propelling it quickly out of sight. We accelerate to catch up with the creature and measure its speed — 60 meters per second! Wow!

MOLLUSK: Mollusks are soft-bodied invertebrates that usually have shells. Mollusks have bilateral symmetry and a fluid-filled body cavity that provides space for the body organs.

There are three classes of mollusks: gastropods, bivalves, and cephalopods.

Gastropods are the largest class of mollusks and include snails, slugs, and conches. Except for slugs, each member of the gastropod class has a single shell. Slugs are protected by a layer of mucus. Many astropods have a pair of tentacles with eyes at the tips. They obtain food by scraping algae and other food materials off rocks. All gastropods move by secreting a layer of mucus and sliding the foot in a series of muscular contractions.

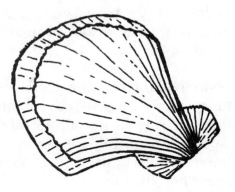

Scallops are one type of Mollusk

Mollusks that have a two-part shell hooked together by a hinge are called bivalves. These animals pull their shells closed with powerful muscles and open their shells by relaxing these muscles. Clams, oysters, and scallops are examples. For protection, clams burrow themselves in the sand with their muscular foot. Oysters cement themselves against solid surfaces to prevent being washed away. Scallops escape predators by opening and shutting their shells quickly. As the water is pushed out, it moves the scallop in the opposite direction. These are the animals we startled earlier.

Cephalopods, which include the squid and octopus, are the most specialized and complex members of the mollusk phylum. They have a large, well-developed head and nervous system, with large eyes similar to human eyes. Their "foot" is divided into many tentacles with strong suckers for capturing prey.

Cephalopods move quickly by jet propulsion. Water is forced out through an opening near the head, sending the organism the opposite direction. A squid or octopus can move very quickly this way for a short amount of time.

We have stopped tracking the octopus, and have rotated the ship to look at the ocean floor. We see two interesting things. The first is a fan of arms that looks like a colorful feather duster. The feathery arms stick out of a white tube inserted in the ocean floor and wave with the motions of the ocean. As our ship passes by, the arms disappear into the tubes.

Another organism is moving across the ocean floor. This animal is fiery orange, with white bristles outlining its entire body. The body is long and segmented. What is this creature?

ANNELID: The word "annelid" means "little rings" and describes the many sections that make up the bodies of segmented worms. Annelids also have a body cavity that holds their organs. Segmented worms include three classes of organisms: earthworms, leeches, and marine worms. The two organisms that we saw, the fan worm and the bristleworm, are examples of marine worms.

Earthworms have a tubelike body with more than 100 segments. They move using bristle-like hairs called **setae.** Each body segment, except for the anterior and posterior segments, has four pairs of setae. To obtain food, earth-

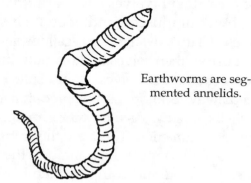

Earthworms are segmented annelids.

worms eat soil, digesting bits of leaves and other organic matter in the soil. Undigested soil and waste materials leave the worm through the anus.

Leeches are not as round or long as earthworms, and they do not have setae. Leeches have two suckers, one at each end of the body, which they use to attach themselves to an animal. Leeches feed on the blood of ducks, fish, and even humans.

Marine worms make up the bulk of annelids. More than 6,000 species have been discovered. These worms have segments with setae. Aside from these common characteristics, there is a great diversity in this class. There are marine worms that can produce their own light, build tubes for retreating, float in the ocean, or walk along the ocean floor. Marine worms come in all shapes, sizes and colors.

We will have to travel to land again, though we will not travel far from the ocean. As we shrink ourselves to a small size once again, we bump into something soft and sticky. All of sudden, our windows are blackened. The ship shakes and shudders. Apparently our ship has been pounced upon by some animal. In our front window, we see two sharp fangs lowering down on us. The fangs press in on the window, but lucky for us, the ship is a strong fortress. The creature rotates and tries again in another spot. Then it jumps to a strong set of cables and crawls up into a corner, eyeing us with its eight eyes. It has a round, raised rump, and a smaller head. Eight legs surround it. What has happened?

ARTHROPOD: The largest phylum in the animal kingdom is made up of arthropods. Insects and spiders are included in this group. In fact, as you might have guessed, the close call we just experienced was an attack from a spider. You'll learn more about spiders as you read about this interesting phyla of animals.

The bodies of arthropods have three sections: the head, the thorax, and the abdomen. These creatures also have a brain, a nervous system, a body cavity, a digestive system, and an **exoskele-**

ton. An exoskeleton is an external covering that covers, supports, and protects the body. There are several classes of arthropods.

Insects are the only invertebrates that are able to fly. Most insects have one or two pairs of wings. They also have a head with a pair of antennae, eyes, and a mouth; a thorax with three pairs of legs; and an abdomen.

Spiders, scorpions, mites, and ticks are arachnids. These invertebrates have only two body regions

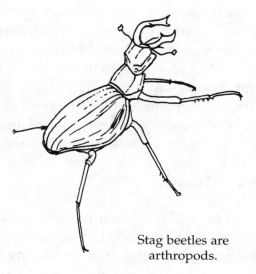

Stag beetles are arthropods.

— a head-chest region and an abdomen. They have four pairs of legs and no antennae. Arachnids kill prey with poison glands, stingers, or fangs.

Centipedes and millipedes have long bodies with many segments, jointed legs, antennae, simple eyes, and exoskeletons. Centipedes have one pair of legs per segment. They are predators and have a pair of poison claws used to inject venom into their prey. Millipedes have two pairs of legs per segment and they feed on plants.

Crustaceans include crabs, crayfish, lobsters, shrimp, and many more. These arthropods have one or two antennae and jaws used for crushing food. Four pairs of legs are used for walking and the fifth pair are claws that catch and hold food. Most live in water. Crustaceans can grow new legs if they happen to lose one in a process called **regeneration.**

Try to find these arthropods in the wild or look them up in an encyclopedia, and then fill in the chart below.

Anthropod Chart

Common Name	# of Legs	# of Body Regions	# of Wings	Name of Group	Special Features
Centipede					
Millipede					
Spider				Arachnids	
Dragonfly					
Butterfly					
Housefly		3			
Tick					
Ladybug	6				
Blue Crab					
Stag Beetle					

Back to the ocean. We are near the shore at the bottom of the ocean. We see a star-shaped organism that is a brilliant blue. Thousands of tube feet line the underside. The creature has found a clam. Using its tube feet, it opens the clam. The shell opens slightly, and the inner part of the star-shaped creature pushes out and surrounds the soft body of the mollusk, secreting a substance over it. Slowly, the clam is digested. The inner part of the starfish pulls its organs back into itself, releases the empty clam, and swims away.

ECHINODERM: Echinoderms include sea stars, sand dollars, and sea urchins. Most of these organisms have radial symmetry, and a spiny skin that covers an internal skeleton. They also have a water-vascular system, a unique network of water-filled canals. As water moves into and out of the system, tube feet act like suction cups and help the echinoderm to move and feed. Echinoderms have four classes: sea stars, brittle stars, sea urchins and sand dollars, and sea cucumbers.

Sea stars have five or more arms arranged around a central point. To feed, a sea star will use its tube feet to manipulate an animal, then it turns its stomach inside out and surrounds the body, digests the animal, and pulls its stomach back inside its body. Sea stars can also grow a new arm if one is lost. Brittle stars move more quickly than sea stars. They will also break off their arms as a defense and can easily grow new parts.

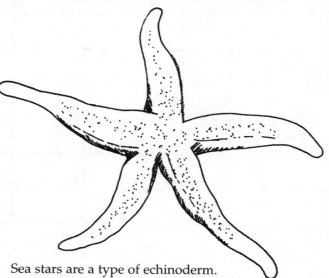

Sea stars are a type of echinoderm.

Both sea urchins and sand dollars are covered with spines. Sand dollars are flat and have small, fine spines. Sea urchins are round and covered with longer spines that poke out in all directions.

Sea cucumbers are different from the other echinoderms.

They have bilateral symmetry rather than radial, and a leathery covering rather than spiny. They have tentacles around the mouth and rows of tube feet that move the sea cucumber along the ocean bottom. This organism may expel its internal organs, if threatened, and regenerate them in a few weeks.

Activity: Go on a nature walk and take a notebook. List all the invertebrates that you see. Afterwards, categorize your list by placing each invertebrate in the correct phylum.

We will now explore another part of the animal kingdom. Many of these animals we know well, but there are some that are as unique as the ones we have already read about. Let's visit the world of vertebrates!

Section 13-4: Vertebrates

The last phylum which we will discuss is called the chordates. All vertebrates are included in this group. Earlier we talked about how all vertebrates have a backbone. This phylum includes most of the animals we know by name. Many of our childhood songs and stories are about them. With chants of "lions, and tigers, and bears, oh my!", readings of Aesop's Fables or The Three Little Pigs, and songs of "Old McDonald had a Farm, " we grow up seeing pictures and imitating the sounds of this group of animals that all have a backbone. Some vertebrates we love; others we fear. Some are extremely useful to us; others are fascinating to observe. The important point is that all have their place in God's creation.

There are eight classes of vertebrates: three classes of fish, and one class each of amphibians, reptiles, birds, and mammals. Let's briefly explore these classes.

We will now visit a mighty river. Throughout this river, trout are abundant. We see one, two, then three of them swim by. The fourth one seems to have an interesting appendage attached to its side. As we look closer, we see that this is not an outgrowth of the fish, but another fish that has attached to the trout with its mouth. Long and tubelike, this fish has smooth and slimy skin, without scales. It seems to be getting its nourishment from the blood of the trout.

FISH: Fish, along with amphibians and reptiles, are vertebrates that are ectotherms. Ectotherms are animals whose internal body temperatures change with the temperature of their surroundings. Fish are specially designed for living in water. They have gills for breathing. They also have hard, thin, overlapping plates called scales that cover the skin and protect the body. Most fish have fins, which are used for steering, balancing, and moving.

The fish group is divided into three classes. Jawless fish include the lampreys and hagfish. These fish have round mouths, no scales, and long, tubelike bodies. The cartilaginous fish include sharks, skates, and rays. These fish have movable jaws and scales. All three are predators. They eat other organisms for food. Both of these classes have skeletons made of **cartilage,** a tough, flexible tissue that is not as hard as bone. The third class of fish is made up of bony fish. These fish have skeletons made of bone. They make up about 95 percent of all species of fish.

We will travel upriver and follow one of its tributaries until we reach a small stream. We notice an insect hovering over the water. All of sudden, a pink flash of something snatches it out of the air. What was that?

AMPHIBIANS: That pink flash was a frog's tongue, snatching up an insect. Frogs are members of the amphibian class. Amphibian means "double life." They are designed to spend part of their lives in water and part on land. A frog is a typical amphibian. It begins as an egg in water. It then grows into a young, legless tadpole. The tadpole grows legs, but continues to feed on plants in the water. The young frog continues to grow until it has the necessary structures for life on land. Adult frogs usually return to the water to lay their eggs.  This process is called **metamorphosis,** a series of changes that an organism goes through to become mature.

Amphibians have moist, smooth, thin skin, without scales. Oxygen and carbon dioxide are exchanged through the skin. They also have small, simple lungs that aid in breathing. They have a strong skeleton made of bone. Land animals need stronger skeletons because they do not have the support of water around them.

Amphibians are ectotherms. Their body temperatures change with their environment. When it is cold, they become inactive, burying themselves in mud or leaves. This is called **hibernation.** Amphibians that live in hot, dry environments become inactive when the hot temperatures become extreme. This is called **estivation.**

Frogs, toads, and salamanders are all examples of amphibians. As adults, frogs and toads have short, broad bodies with no neck or tail. The two strong hind legs are longer than the front legs and are used for swimming and jumping. Bulging eyes and nostrils on top of the head let frogs and toads see and breathe while they are almost totally submerged in water. Frogs eat mostly insects. A frog's tongue is attached to the front of its mouth. When it sees an insect, it flips the loose end of its tongue out and catches the insect with the frog's sticky saliva. The frog flips its tongue back into its mouth and swallows the insect. Toads eat spiders, earthworms, and caterpillars. Most toads have thick, warty skin, and glands on their backs that secrete poison.

Salamanders and newts are amphibians that have long, slender bodies, and short legs that stick straight out from the sides of their bodies. They feed at night, eating worms, crustaceans, and insects. During the day, they hide under rocks and leaves to escape the sun. Salamanders usually breed on land.

Activity: Look at the diagram below. List the stages of metamorphosis beginning with the egg stage, and ending with the adult frog stage.

Amphibian Metamorphosis

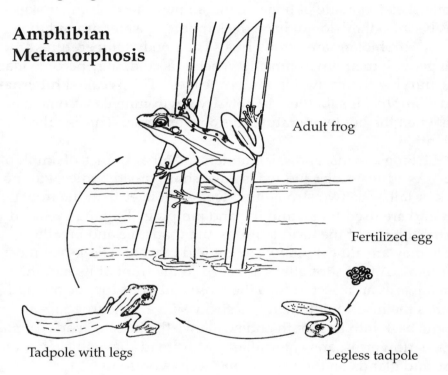

Adult frog

Fertilized egg

Tadpole with legs

Legless tadpole

1. The egg stage

2. _____

3. _____

4. Adult frog stage

Shhh! A hunter is prowling through the swamps of this jungle. The swamp is shaded with the long limbs of trees that reach over the water. We look in the water. A log is floating on the surface of the algae-covered, muddy water. It is hot and humid. The air feels heavy. Our eyes turn to the log again. Our gaze travels over the length of it, and you see two eyes blinking at the end. That is not a log! A grazing animal nears the water. We watch the "log" move slowly, silently, towards the beast. As it passes under an overhanging limb, a large, serpentine creature drops on top of it. The two animals sink beneath the surface, and then there is a thrashing of the water, followed by silence. You watch in amazement as the ten-meter-long creature swallows the crocodile whole.

REPTILES: Who was the hunter on the prowl? The croco-dile was prowling, yes, but it was the giant python who got the kill. Both of these predators are examples of reptiles. A reptile is an ectothermic vertebrate with dry, scaly skin. Reptiles differ from amphibians in that they do not need water in order to reproduce. Reptiles breathe with lungs. The class of reptiles includes extinct dinosaurs, but today there are three orders of reptiles: turtles, crocodiles and alligators, and lizards and snakes.

Turtles are covered by a hard shell on both top and bottom. Most turtles can withdraw into their shells for protection. Turtles have no teeth and use their beaks to feed on insects, worms, fish, and plants.

Crocodiles and alligators can be found in or near water in tropical climates. Crocodiles have long, slender snouts and are more aggressive than alligators. They can attack animals as large as cattle. Alligators feed on fish, turtles, and waterbirds.

Lizards have movable eyelids, external ears, and legs with clawed toes on each foot. They feed on reptiles, insects, spiders, worms, and mammals. Snakes do not have legs, eyelids, or external ears. They sense vibrations in the ground through their lower jawbone. Snakes are meat eaters. Many help control the rodent population by feeding on them. Farmers often welcome these rodent-eaters. Snakes kill their prey in different ways. Some are constrictors — they wrap their bodies around their prey and suffocate them. Others inject their prey with venom.

Reptile

Activity: Describe a pet that you or somebody you know has owned, without naming the animal or the class in which it belongs. Was it an endotherm or ectotherm? Describe its skin, shape of body features, its feeding habits, and other distinguishing characteristics. Give your description to a friend and have them guess what it is.

Now we will fly up into the air. We rise up, up, up the side of a mountain and beyond it. Below us are the arid foothills and mountains of southern and central California. Far below, we can see an eagle, circling over its nest site in a rocky crag on the mountain top. We know that we are high up when we look down at the eagles. But wait! There is another flying object in the air beside us. As we focus our spotting scope on this bird, we are amazed at its size — it has a nine-foot wingspan. The wings are black with white wing linings that contrast with its burnt orange, featherless head. It has only one eye, and a curved, white beak. It soars on flat wings, circling for altitude, then gives one deep wingbeat and soars off at a great speed.

BIRDS: What we have just seen is an amazing event. The California condor has almost died out as a species in California. The condor we saw must be the successful result of a captive breeding program. The California condor is an amazing bird, known not only for its immense size, but also for its soaring ability. Pilots of airplanes have reported sighting the birds at incredible heights.

The California condor is part of the class of birds. Birds are vertebrates. However, unlike fish, amphibians, and reptiles, they are **endotherms** — animals that have a constant internal body temperature. Also unlike the other classes, birds care for their young. Fish, amphibians, and most reptiles lay their eggs and leave them. Birds keep their eggs warm until hatched, and then continue to feed them until they become mature.

The main characteristic about birds that most people notice is that birds have wings, and most have the ability to fly. Birds are the only class of the animal kingdom that has feathers. A bird's body is covered by two types of feathers, contour feathers and down feathers. Contour feathers are strong, lightweight, and have a smooth, sleek shape. These are the feathers that give a bird its color and enable it to fly. Soft, fluffy down feathers provide insulation and help birds to maintain their constant body temperature.

There are almost 9,000 species of birds with a wide variety of

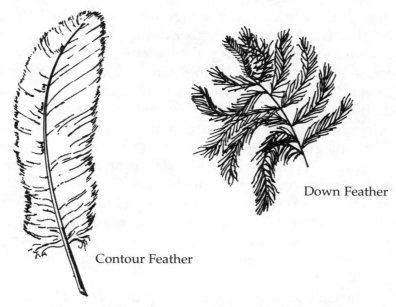

Contour Feather

Down Feather

features are displayed. Some cannot fly, but are fast runners. Other have webbed feet used for swimming. There are birds with long, thin legs used for wading, or strong claws for grasping and tearing.

      If you look at the diagram on the following page, you will also see some examples of how the beaks of birds are different. Predator birds have sharp, hooked beaks for tearing flesh. Perching birds have long pointed beaks for boring into wood to find insects. Seed-eating birds have short, thick, strong beaks for cracking seeds. Wading birds have large beaks for snatching and swallowing fish. God has carefully designed each and every one of them.

Many people observe birds for sport. Bird-watchers carry bird guides, binoculars, and spotting scopes to observe birds closely and identify them. Bird-watchers usually keep lists of how

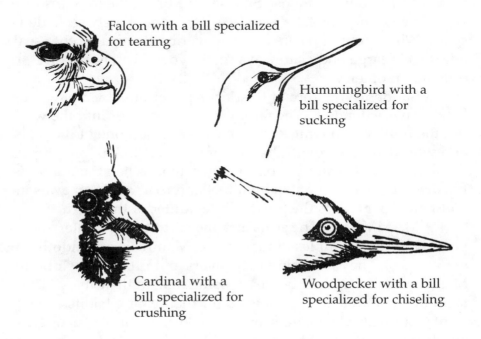

Falcon with a bill specialized for tearing

Hummingbird with a bill specialized for sucking

Cardinal with a bill specialized for crushing

Woodpecker with a bill specialized for chiseling

many different species of birds they have identified in the wild.

Activity: Go on a nature walk and try to identify the birds around you. If you are unable to identify a bird, write a description of it in a notebook. Note the call, the colors of its different feathers, and its size. Also describe the color and shape of its beak and legs, and the environment in which you found it. If possible, include descriptions of the markings around its eyes, face, and body. Then go to the library and look it up in a bird guide. If you enjoy this activity, consider buying a pair of binoculars and a bird guide, and start an identified bird-list of your own!

We will now steer towards the icy north. It is a beautiful, pristine world. West of us is a majestic mountain range. A frozen lake stretches out before us. Silence. We break the ice barrier, and sink down under the lake's surface. We immediately see a den of seals. With a roof of packed snow covering them, a mother seal adjusts her large body sideways so her young can nurse. It is a touching moment.

Suddenly, the roof of the den is penetrated by a paw with black claws extended. The family of seals scurries into the water, but the hunter is too quick. The paw scoops up one of the seals and whisks it up through the roof of the den. Before our ship can surface, the seal is almost completely eaten. When the hunter is finished, it stands up on its hind feet and roars. It is an awesome and fierce giant. It is the great, white hunter of the north.

MAMMALS: The seals and the great white hunter, the polar bear, are examples of mammals. Mammals are endothermic vertebrates. They have skin that covers and protects their bodies. Most have hair on their bodies at some time in their lives. The teeth of a mammal are specialized for their eating habits. Large front teeth help plant eaters, or herbivores, to cut blades of grass and leaves of plants. Sharp pointed teeth help meat eaters, or carnivores, to rip and tear flesh. Omnivores eat both plants and animals. Mammals are active. All have four-chambered hearts that pump blood directly to the body, and well-developed lungs.

Like birds, all mammals provide care for their young. Unlike birds, mammals produce milk to feed their young. Mammals are classified into three groups based on how their young develop.

Monotremes are mammals that lay eggs with tough, leathery shells. When the young hatch, they nurse by licking milk from the skin and hair surrounding the female's mammary glands. The duckbilled platypus is probably the most well-known monotreme.

Marsupials are pouched animals that give birth to tiny, immature offspring. Immediately after birth, the young offspring crawls into the pouch on the female's abdomen and attaches to a nipple. It remains protected in the pouch while it feeds and develops more completely. When it is more mature, it will leave the pouch for short periods of time. Kangaroos and opossums are well-known examples of marsupials.

Placental mammals develop inside the female in the uterus. These mammals are named for the sack-like organ surrounding the growing embryo called the placenta. An umbilical cord attaches the embryo to the placenta. It transports food and oxygen to the embryo and takes waste products away from it. The diversity of this group of mammals is great. Bats, moles, squirrels, rabbits, horses, camels, bears, elephants, whales, and humans are all included in this group. Manatees, armadillos, lemurs, hyraxes, pangolins, and aardvarks are examples of some of the lessknown orders of placental mammals.

Section 13-5: Ecology

Then God blessed them, and God said to them, "Be fruitful and multiply; fill the earth and subdue it; have dominion over the fish of the sea, over the birds of the air, and over every living thing that moves on the earth." And God said, "See, I have given you every herb... and every tree... to you it shall be for food...."
Genesis 1:28,29

God loaned us the earth. He told us to fill it and use it. He gave us power over the wild beasts, so they would be afraid of us. He gave us every herb, tree, and plant to use. Yet the world is still the Lord's. God reminds us in the scriptures that the gold and silver are His, the mountains and rivers, the weather, and the beasts that walk upon it and swim in the waters. All of these things are His.

You have probably heard of the word "steward." A steward is somebody who cares for another's possessions or property. When the owner returns, the steward must answer for the condition of what was entrusted to him. We are stewards of God's earth. We must care for it as something that has been entrusted to us. God has loaned us the earth to us. If we abuse it, we are abusing God's property and possessions. We will have to answer for it sometime, now or in heaven. Or worse, our children will reap the punishment for our mistakes. As we read about the balance that is created in the relationships between organisms and the environment, think about ways in which we can better care for this great gift God has loaned us — the earth.

The science of **ecology** is the study of the relationships between organisms and the environment. An **organism** is an individual living thing. Organisms that live in the same place and can produce young form a population. A **population** is all of the individuals of one species living in the same area at the same time.

These populations usually do not live alone. Populations of different species interact with other populations to form a **community.** An **ecosystem** consists of communities and the environmental factors that affect them. All the ecosystems on the earth make up what is called the **biosphere,** the part of the earth that supports living organisms.

Ecologists are scientists who study the relationships between organisms and the environment. We will first look at the relationship between organisms. Most of the interactions between organisms of different species are feeding relationships.

A simple way of showing a feeding relationship among a group of animals is a **food chain.** When drawing a food chain, arrows between organisms point to the consumer. **Consumers** are organisms that obtain food when they feed on other consumers or producers. **Producers** are organisms that make their own food, such as plankton, algae, and other plants. The food chain always begins with a producer. An herbivore, or animal that eats plants, eats the producer. The herbivore is eaten by a carnivore, or meat-eater. A carnivore that eats other carnivores is called a top carnivore. A typical food chain might look like this:

algae (producer)—>insect (herbivore)—>frog (carnivore)—>snake (top carnivore)

Food chains are really too simple a way to describe the many interactions between organisms in an ecosystem. A more complete way of describing the feeding relationships between organisms is a food web. If you look at the food web on the next page, you will see better how the organisms interact.

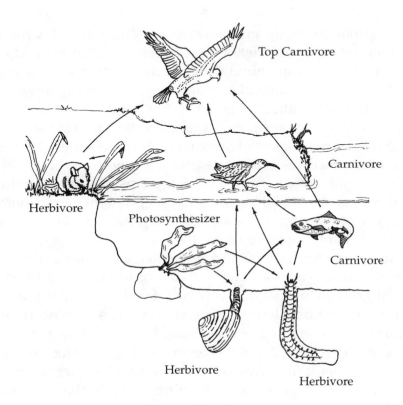

Top Carnivore

Carnivore

Carnivore

Herbivore

Photosynthesizer

Herbivore

Herbivore

Look at the diagram above. Create a food chain that might exist among these characters.

Ecologists also study the relationships between organisms and their environment. A pond ecosystem is made of algae, insects, amphibians, birds, and other living things that depend on one another for food. However, these organisms also depend on nonliving factors that surround them, such as water, soil, sunlight, temperature, and air. We will explore these different nonliving factors and how they affect organisms.

Water is an important environmental factor. Almost all the bodies of organisms consist of 50 percent or more water. Important life processes such as respiration, photosynthesis, and digestion can only occur with water. Soil helps to determine the type of plants and other organisms that will inhabit a certain area. Most soil is a combination of sand, clay, and humus. The greater the humus content, the more fertile the soil.

Light and temperature also impact an ecosystem. The availability of sunlight is a major factor in determining where green plants will grow. This factor in turn affects what animals will be attracted to the region. Temperature also impacts an ecosystem. For instance, as we learned in the water chapter, the deepest parts of the ocean are extremely cold. The pressure and lack of sunlight also make it difficult for living things to exist. Only organisms that can withstand these extreme conditions live in this ecosystem.

Chapter 13 Review

1) In which order did God create the animals?

2) What are two defining characteristics of animals that are also defining characteristics of plants?

3) Compare invertebrates and vertebrates.

4) Compare the three types of symmetry.

5) What is a filter feeder?

6) What does the word "cnidaria" mean?

7) Describe the relationship of a parasite and its host. Compare a parasite with a free-living organism.

8) Roundworms are the cause of what common disease in dogs?

9) List and describe the three classes of mollusks.

10) What does the word "annelid" mean? Give two examples of an annelid.

11) Define exoskeleton. Which phylum contains animals with exoskeletons?

12) Define regeneration. Name two phyla that are able to regenerate.

13) Describe the unique water-vascular system of echinoderms.

14) Compare ectotherms with endotherms.

15) Name the three classes of fish.

16) What does the word "amphibian" mean? Why is this an appropriate name for the class?

17) Compare hibernation and estivation.

18) How do reptiles differ from amphibians?

19) Compare lizards and snakes.

20) Name three characteristics of birds that separate them from fish, amphibians and reptiles.

21) Name three defining characteristics of mammals.

22) How do mammals differ from birds in the care for their young?

23) Give an example of a monotreme, marsupial, and placental mammal.

Student Objectives
Chapter 14: The Human Body

My objectives are:

1. I will memorize the skin's major parts and label them on a diagram.

2. I will measure the surface area of my skin.

3. I will memorize the parts of a nerve cell and label them on a diagram.

4. I will sort several words according to the sense with which they are associated.

5. I will memorize the major parts of the circulatory system and label them on a diagram.

6. I will calculate how many times my heart beats in a day.

7. I will measure my lung capacity and compare it with that of a partner.

8. I will memorize the major parts of the respiratory system and label them on a diagram.

9. I will memorize the major parts of the digestive system and label them on a diagram.

10. I will observe my dietary habits and compare them with the food pyramid.

Chapter 14: The Human Body

For you have formed my inward parts; You have covered me in my mother's womb. I will praise You, for I am fearfully and wonderfully made; Marvelous are Your works, And that my soul knows very well. My frame was not hidden from You, When I was made in secret, And skillfully wrought in the lowest parts of the earth. Your eyes saw my substance, being yet unformed.

Psalm 139:13-16

We have been to some amazing places and seen some incredible sights. From the atom to the star; from the crystal, white icy lands to the colorful, brilliant rain forests of earth; from the Portuguese man-of-war with its stinging strands to the still, tall, evergreen pine tree; we have seen many sizes, colors and shapes of God's creation. And even though we have traveled in a ship that can travel light-years in a matter of seconds, dodge asteroids and defend itself from spider attacks, shrink and enlarge itself to whatever size we need, we still have not even begun to make a dent in the discovery of all that God has made. We could continue traveling for a millennium, and still feel there is more to explore than what we have already studied. That should not discourage us, but fill us with anticipation. Exploration is fun! The more we explore, the more we learn about the Creator who made it all.

Now we will turn to ourselves. As the verse at the top of the page notes, we are "fearfully and wonderfully made." We are the only earthly beings which were designed in the image of God. We are the only parts of creation for which Jesus Christ died. Throughout the history of mankind, we have been sought after, provided for, and loved by the Creator of this vast universe. As we study the human body, note just how wonderfully we are made. Also, take time to reflect on how the spirit that God gave to each of us is really a place that cannot be explored by our ship, but only through a relationship with the One who designed us. A quote by St. Augustine provides an apt summary: "Men go abroad to wonder at the height of mountains, at the huge waves of the sea, at the long courses of the rivers, at the vast compass of the ocean, at the circular motion of the stars; and they pass by themselves without wondering."

Section 14-1: Skin

The first place we will study is the body's largest organ, the skin. As we near the skin, we notice large flakes falling all around us. As we penetrate the skin, we see that the skin is covered in this flaky substance. Next we see many plump cells surrounding us. As we push through into a new layer, we see all sorts of strange sights. A huge, black shaft is to our left. Tiny, rubbery branches are everywhere. Large tubes serve as a vehicle to move red and blue liquids. There is a huge pond filled with a sticky substance to our right. Behind us there is a mess of coiled tubing filled with a clear liquid. We continue to move inward, and enter a new layer. Thousands and thousands of yellowish balls surround us. What are we seeing? Let's find out.

The first layer of skin is called the **epidermis.** The thousands of flakes we saw were the dead skin cells that are constantly being rubbed off. The epidermis is covered with dead skin cells. Underneath new cells are constantly being produced that eventually replace the ones that are rubbed off.

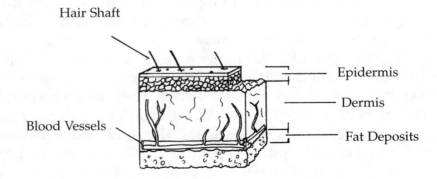

Hair Shaft

Blood Vessels

Epidermis

Dermis

Fat Deposits

The **dermis** is the next layer in our skin. This layer is thicker than the epidermis. We saw many interesting things within the dermis. The huge, black shaft is a hair follicle. The rubbery branches are nerve endings that help us to feel heat or cold, pressure, or textures. The tubes of red and blue liquids are blood vessels transporting blood to and from the heart. The pond of the sticky substance is an oil gland, and the mess of coiled tubing is a sweat gland. Underneath the dermis is a layer of fat cells that help to insulate our bodies.

We have learned about all the parts of the skin. However, it is also important to know the functions of the skin's parts. God designed skin to perform various tasks for the body.

PROTECTION: Probably the most important function of skin is the protection it provides your body. It covers the body and protects it from physical injury. It also guards the body from bacteria, viruses, diseases, and infection. Skin also holds important things inside the body, such as water.

SENSE: When reading about the branches of nerve endings, we learned that these parts help us to feel temperature, pressure and pain. Perhaps you wonder why feeling pain is important. Pain is important because it helps us to avoid dangers to our bodies. If we did not feel anything when we touched a hot stove, we might seriously damage our body by leaning on it. Pain helps us to jump away from the hot stove.

BODY TEMPERATURE: As we learned in the previous chapter, the human is a mammal. One of the main characteristics of mammals is that they are endotherms. They have a constant body temperature. The skin of a human plays an important role in helping to regulate body temperature. The layer of fat cells insulates our bodies. It helps to keep our bodies at a constant temperature. The skin's sweat glands help to cool our bodies if we become overheated. There are about three million sweat glands in the dermis. These glands release heat through pores in the skin. The perspiration moves out onto the skin, and the body cools as the sweat evaporates.

EXCRETE WASTES: Sweat glands also help our bodies get rid of wastes. Sweat glands release water, salt, and a protein called urea.

Health note: Skin cancer is on the rise in America. To avoid skin cancer, it is important to avoid being burned by the sun. Always wear a good layer of sunscreen when planning on being in the sun for a long period of time. Also, consistently check your body for moles. If any new ones appear, or old ones change color, shape, or size, visit a doctor to check it. Skin cancer is very preventable. If left unchecked, however, it is very dangerous.

Look at the diagram of the skin on page 391. After you have memorized the parts of the skin, test yourself on the blank diagram below.

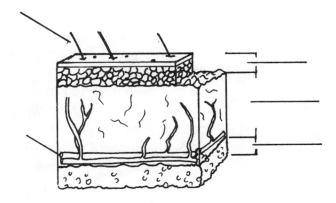

Activity: The surface area of your skin
Materials: newspapers, scissors, tape, tape measure, and string
Hypothesis: How much surface area does my skin cover?

Procedure:
1. Measure the length of your arm and the distance around it.
2. Cut out two (one for each arm) identical pieces of newspaper that correspond to these two lengths.
3. Measure the length of your leg and the distance around it.
4. Cut out two (one for each leg) identical pieces of newspaper that correspond to these two lengths.
5. Measure the length of your torso and the distance around it.
6. Cut out one piece of newspaper that corresponds to this length.
7. Lay out the pieces of newspaper on the floor.
8. Observe how much surface area your skin covers.
9. How much does the actual surface area of your skin and the amount you guessed differ?

Section 14-2: The Nervous System

      We are sitting somewhere behind the eye. We are extremely tiny. I'm not quite sure what we are sitting on. The ship's gauges have not pinpointed our exact location yet. Whoa! We are on what seems like the fastest, biggest roller coaster of our lives. We shoot up quickly, then take a long plunge that seems to go on forever. We level out and shoot horizontally to who knows where, and stop suddenly. What happened?

      Let's examine the events we just experienced. Our ship's gauges have created a map of our whereabouts, as well as a list of the places we have just visited. We visited the brain, shot down the spinal cord and out to an arm. Yes, it is as I suspected. We were riding an impulse. Very entertaining now that it is all over. We are in the nervous system of the body!

      The nervous system is grouped into two major divisions: **the central nervous system (CNS)** and the **peripheral nervous system (PNS).** The central nervous system is composed of the brain and the spinal cord. The peripheral nervous system includes all of the nerves outside the central nervous system.

      We must have been inside a nerve cell, or **neuron,** when that impulse shot into motion. A neuron is made up of a cell body. **Dendrites** are branches that receive messages and send them to the cell body. An axon looks like a long tail streaming from the neuron. It carries messages away from the cell body. The message is called an **impulse.** The impulse is transferred from neuron to neuron until the proper response is made by the body.

      Not all neurons are the same. Different neurons have different functions. **Sensory neurons** receive information and send impulses to the brain or spinal cord. We must have started inside a sensory neuron. The human we are visiting must have seen something disturbing, and so his sensory neurons reacted by sending an impulse to the brain. **Interneurons** relay impulses from the sensory nervous to the motor neurons. We must have been traveling through interneurons when we took that enormous plunge down the spinal cord. **Motor neurons** conduct impulses from the brain or spinal cord to muscles or glands throughout the body. When we finished we were riding a motor neuron as the message was sent to muscles to respond.

The ride felt like a roller coaster. However, unlike a roller coaster, which has wheels attached to the tracks, our impulse had to make many jumps across gaps. Neurons do not touch each other. To get from one neuron to another, an impulse moves across a small space called a **synapse.**

Nerve Cell

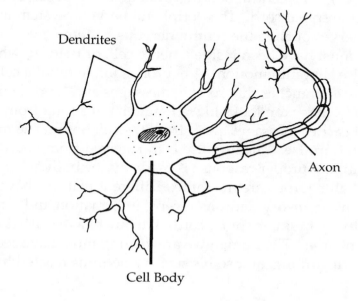

Dendrites

Axon

Cell Body

396

Our entire roller coaster ride was a response to something the human saw. Vision is one of the five senses that our nervous system enables us to have. Our eyes are equipped with two types of cells called rods and cones. Cones respond to bright light and color. Rods respond to dim light. Light energy stimulates impulses in these cells. The impulses pass to the optic nerve, which carries them to the brain. The brain interprets what we "see."

Other nerve cells help us to hear. When an object vibrates, it causes the air around it to vibrate, creating sound waves. When sound waves reach our ears, they stimulate nerve cells deep in the ears. Impulses are sent to the brain, and the brain interprets the sound.

Nasal passages also contain nerve cells called **olfactory cells** that help us to smell. We can smell a flower's fragrance because it gives off molecules into the air. The olfactory cells are stimulated by these molecules, send an impulse to our brains, where it is recognized, or if it is new, remembered and so we can recognize it next time.

Taste is another sense that is made possible because of nerve cells. When we think of food, our mouths begin to water with saliva. This adaptation is helpful because, in order to taste something, it has to be dissolved in water. The solution washes over the sensory receptors that are called **taste buds,** and an impulse is sent to our brains. The brain interprets the impulse, and we identify the taste.

About 10,000 taste buds are found all over our tongues. The taste buds are grouped in different places on our tongues and help us to distinguish between different tastes. The taste buds at the tip of our tongues help us to taste sweet things. Located behind this area are groups of taste buds that help us taste things that are salty. Behind those, are taste buds that help us taste things that are sour. At the back of our tongue is an area that helps us taste bitter things.

Health Note: The nervous system is easily affected by what you put into your body. Alcohol is a depressant. It slows down the activities of the central nervous system. Had we traveled on an impulse from a drunk person, perhaps our adventure would have felt like a pleasure cruise rather than a roller coaster ride. Judgment, reasoning, memory, and concentration are impaired. Heavy use of alcohol eventually destroys brain cells making the damage permanent.

Caffeine, on the other hand, is a stimulant. It speeds up the activities of the central nervous system. Too much caffeine can increase heartbeat rate and cause restlessness. People can become addicted to caffeine as well as to alcohol. When people stop taking caffeine, they often experience headaches and nausea. You may be thinking, "I don't drink coffee." Many soft drinks have the same amount of caffeine, if not more, than a cup of coffee.

Your body has a more difficult time responding the way it is supposed to under the effects of drugs. Think before you drink!

Each of the following words is associated with one of the five senses of your body. In the table on the following page are five columns with the name of each sense at the top. Write words that are associated with a certain sense in the correct column.

whisper	smelly	dim	cold	smooth
fragrant	colorful	sweet	blink	hot
salty	sour	small	bitter	squint
loud	bright	velvety	noisy	buzz
rough	sharp	large	odor	glasses

Smell	Touch	Hearing	Sight	Taste

Section 14-3: The Muscular System

Now we will examine another system in the body. Before us is a large amount of tissue. It has a striped appearance, and is attached to a large, white shaft with bands of tissue. Suddenly, the tissue begins to pull and become more compact. We feel ourselves being lifted and then dropped.

What we are seeing is a muscle at work. A **muscle** is an organ that pulls and gets shorter, providing the force needed to move our body parts. Muscles that we can control are called voluntary muscles. The movement of our arms and legs are examples of using **voluntary muscles.** The muscles in your face are also voluntary. We are able to control them by smiling, frowning, or making other facial expressions.

Muscles that we cannot control are called **involuntary muscles.** These muscles move and work without our thinking about them. For instance, blood is pumped from our hearts without our consciously telling them to pump. Our digestive system moves food throughout our bodies without us havoing to be reminded.

Not all muscles look the same. The one we saw in motion was an example of a skeletal muscle. **Skeletal muscles** are the ones that move bones. They are attached to bones by thick bands of tissue called tendons. These muscles have a striped appearance. Skeletal muscles are voluntary muscles. We control when they move. These muscles contract quickly, but become tired very easily.

Smooth muscles are involuntary muscles. They move many of our internal organs. Our blood vessels are made of smooth muscle. Their name hints to us that these muscles are not striped, as skeletal muscles are, but have a smooth appearance. These muscles contract and relax slowly.

Cardiac muscle is found only in the heart. Like skeletal muscles, this type of muscle has a striped appearance. Like smooth muscles, however, cardiac muscle is involuntary. Cardiac muscle moves all the time, every day. Every heartbeat is a result of our cardiac muscle contracting.

Health Note: Exercise is an important part of being healthy. A disciplined person will include exercise as a part of his or her life. Those who have sedentary habits, such as sitting in front of the television, computer, or a book all the time, will eventually suffer in their muscular system. The muscles will become soft and flabby, and will lack strength. Muscles that aren't exercised become smaller in size. Combine this with bad eating habits, and obesity is likely to occur. A disciplined life will reflect a balance between physical and mental activity, and rest. All should be included in our daily habits.

Section 14-4: The Cardiovascular System

We will begin at the heart. With a huge push, we are sent out into the body. We move at a moderate speed in a series of pushes. It looks as if we are driving through a complex highway system. Everywhere we look, the roads before us are branching in different directions. Some are small lanes. Others are large, open tunnels.

We are surrounded by liquid filled with bright, red, gel-filled sacs. Push! Push! Push! We see a bend up ahead. There is darkness, and our ship squeezes through a tiny passageway, and passes into another part of the body.

As we begin to move in an upward direction and out of the darkness, we notice that the color of our surroundings has changed. Everywhere there is a bluish tint. We are shoved upwards, and then the tunnel we are in squeezes behind us. Push! Push! Push! We are pushed through and caught by the squeezing tunnel. Soon we arrive back where we started. The pumping heart is before us. We have completed our journey through the cardiovascular system.

Nutrients and oxygen are distributed throughout the body by means of what is called a **cardiovascular system.** "Cardio-" means "heart," and "vascular" means "vessel." The cardiovascular system includes the heart, blood, and kilometers of vessels that carry blood to every part of the body.

HEART: The heart has four cavities called chambers. The two upper chambers are the right and left **atria.** The two lower chambers are the right and left **ventricles.** During a single heartbeat, both atria contract, followed by both ventricles.

VESSELS: Blood is carried away from the heart by blood vessels called **arteries.** With each contraction of the heart, blood is moved or "pushed" from the heart to the different areas of the body. When blood has completed its journey away from the heart, it passes through microscopic blood vessels called capillaries. The walls of **capillaries** are only one cell thick. This is the transfer station. Nutrients and oxygen move to body cells through thin capillary walls. Waste materials and carbon dioxide move from body cells into the capillaries to be carried back to the heart. **Veins** are blood vessels that move blood to the heart. Backward movement of the blood is prevented by one-way valves that close. Because the blood in these vessels is low in oxygen, it has a bluish tint.

Cardiovascular System

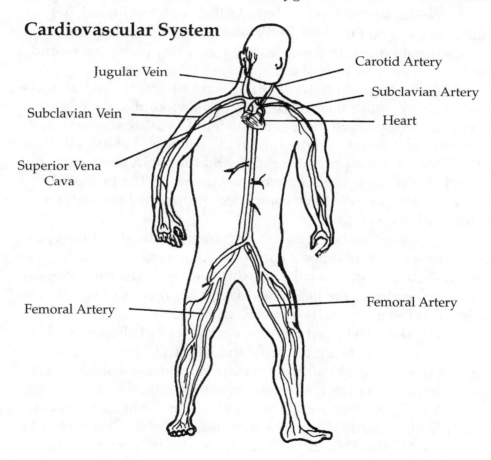

Jugular Vein

Carotid Artery

Subclavian Artery

Subclavian Vein

Heart

Superior Vena Cava

Femoral Artery

Femoral Artery

Look at the diagram of the circulatory system on the previous page. After you have memorized its major parts, test yourself by covering the previous page and filling in the blanks on the diagram below.

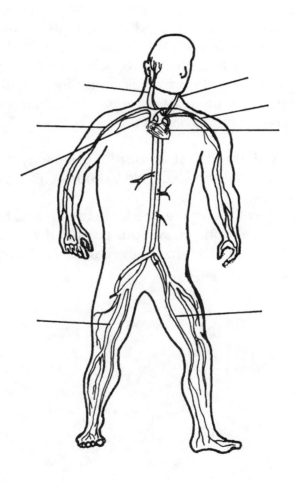

Math Activity: If your heart beats 70 times per minute, how many times does it beat in a day?

Health Note: Heart disease is the major cause of death in the United States. Eating foods high in cholesterol and saturated fats may cause fatty deposits to form on artery walls. The fat eventually clogs the inside of the blood vessels. This condition is called atherosclerosis. Another condition is high blood pressure. When the pressure within vessels increases, the walls lose their ability to contract. The heart has to work harder to keep blood flowing. Being overweight, as well as eating foods with too much salt and fat, may contribute to hypertension. Smoking and stress can also lead to high blood pressure.

Activity: What is your lung capacity?
Materials needed: two balloons and a partner

Procedure: Take one large breath and blow into the balloon. Have your partner do the same. Compare the size of the balloons. A bigger balloon indicates a larger lung capacity.

Section 14-5: The Skeletal System

We are traveling down a long, white, rounded structure. The surface of our pathway is not smooth. There are bumps, edges, round ends, rough spots, and many pits and holes. In several places, tissue is attached to some of the bumps and pits. Many of the holes are filled with tubes and ropes.

The structure on which we are traveling is a bone. This bone, along with all the bones in our bodies, is part of an important bodily system called the skeletal system. The skeleton helps the body in many ways. It gives shape and support to your body. Muscles are attached to bones and help the skeletal system to move your body. Bones protect your internal organs, such as the heart, lungs, and brain. Also, blood cells are formed in the red marrow of some bones. Lastly, major quantities of calcium and phosphorus compounds are stored for later use. These elements are what make bones hard.

Let's examine the interior of a bone. You may be surprised to learn that bone is not dead and lifeless. Even though bones are often associated with death, they are actually made of layers of living tissue. The surface of the bone is covered with a tough, tight-fitting membrane called the **periosteum.** The periosteum contains small blood vessels that carry nutrients into the bone, and cells that help the bone to grow or repair. Beneath the periosteum is a hard, strong layer called **compact bone.** Compact bone contains bone cells, blood vessels, and deposits of calcium and phosphorus. Long bones may have spongy bone at their ends. This helps to make the bone more lightweight. The center of these long bones contain marrow, a fatty tissue that produces red and white blood cells.

A smooth, thick layer of tissue called cartilage covers the

end of a bone. Cartilage is flexible, absorbing shock and reducing friction between bones. Any place where two or more bones meet is a joint. A ligament is a tough band of tissue that holds bones together at joints. The joint is lubricated by a fluid. Joints are places between bones that enable the framework to be flexible.

Health Note: Osteoporosis is a disease that breaks down bone, causing it to become brittle and weak. Many bone fractures are a result of osteoporosis. Also, if you have ever seen an elderly person with a curved spine, he may be suffering from osteoporosis. Some causes of this disease are eating a diet low in calcium, consuming too much caffeine, and getting too little exercise. Calcium is a mineral that the body can store. Begin putting calcium in your calcium "bank" to prevent osteoporosis.

Section 14-6: The Respiratory System

We are outside of the body, floating as a microscopic ship in the air. Suddenly, a vacuum sucks us in through a dark, tunnel. Long branches wave around the ship and stick to it. We move to another tubelike passageway. The windows begin to fog, making it difficult to see. The ship's gauges show that we are surrounded by warm, moist air.

As we move down the passageway, we pass through a flap of tissue. We now see several cords, and sound is emitting from them. We see them stretch and loosen again and again. We enter another tube that has a ribbed lining. It is very windy through here. Downward we go until our passage divides into two short branches. We go to the right. Though we do not leave the tube we are in, we can see through it and realize that we are in an extremely spacious, open cavern.

We continue through the tube, branching this way and that. Each turn brings us into a smaller tunnel. Then we stop. We are surrounded by bright, red disks that surround us and then leave. We transfer to another tiny tube, and begin to head up through the cavern again. Our return journey is similar to our journey in.

We have just traveled through the respiratory system. We were sucked into the body with air through the human's nose. Once inside one of the two nasal passages called **nostrils,** hair traps dust from the air, and helps to filter it. Air then passes to the nasal cavity where it is moistened and warmed.

The warm, moist air moves to the **pharynx,** a tubelike passageway for both food and air. At the lower end of the pharynx is a flap of tissue called the **epiglottis.** The epiglottis closes over the larynx when you swallow to prevent food from entering there. The **larynx** is an airway to which your vocal cords are attached. When you speak, muscles tighten or loosen your vocal cords. The cords vibrate when air moves past, producing sound.

From the larynx, air moves to the **trachea,** a 12-centimeter tube with rings of cartilage. The rings help the trachea to stay open and to prevent it from collapsing. Air moves from the trachea to one of two short branches called **bronchi.** The bronchi are what moved us into the open cavern, which was a lung. Within

Respiratory System

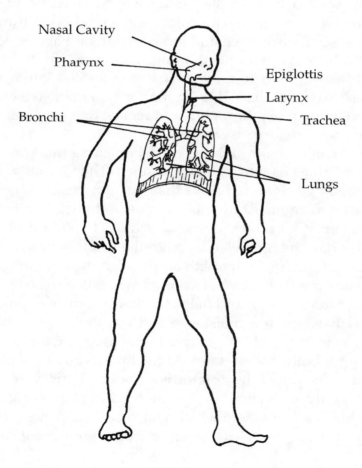

the lungs, the bronchi branch into smaller tubes until they reach the smallest tubes called **bronchioles.** Tiny, thin-walled sacs called alveoli are at the end of each bronchiole. Capillaries surround the alveoli, where the exchange of oxygen and carbon dioxide takes place. There the oxygen is picked up by red blood cells and carried to the rest of the body. Also, carbon dioxide is transported back out of the bodyleaving the body when we exhale.

Look at the diagram of the respiratory system on the previous page. After you have memorized the major parts, test yourself

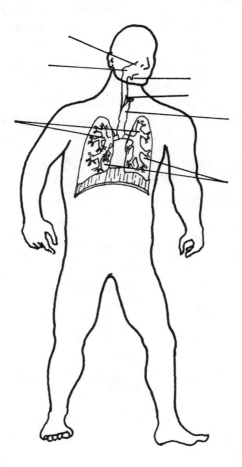

on the blank diagram below.

Health Note: Smoking is the leading cause of most lung diseases. Smoking may cause **chronic bronchitis,** a disease in which the bronchial tubes are irritated for a long time. Eventually bronchial tubes can become damaged, affecting the lungs' ability to move mucus, bacteria, and dirt particles out of the air. Smoking can also cause **emphysema,** a disease in which the alveoli in the lungs lose their ability to expand and contract. As a result, alveoli can't push air out of the lungs. Blood becomes low in oxygen and high in carbon dioxide. Because the heart works harder to supply oxygen to body cells, people who have emphysema often develop heart problems as well.

Smoking is the greatest contributing factor to lung cancer, the leading cause of cancer deaths in men and women in the United States. Smoking is also believed to be a factor in the development of cancer of the mouth, esophagus, larynx, and pancreas.

Smoking cigarettes is very addictive. Many people want to stop smoking, but have extreme difficulties in quitting their addiction. The best way to prevent addiction to cigarettes is to never start smoking them.

Section 14-7: The Digestive System

We are outside of the body once again. We are in a strange land, with white walls that rise up on both sides. Suddenly, we are lifted out of the land, carried through the air upwards, and emptied into a dark, red cave with arched ceilings. It is warm and moist. Then the cave begins to move. Large, white pillars separate and crush together several times, smashing and squashing the substances that are present. Whoa! That was close! The floor lifts; we are squeezed through an opening and slide down a tunnel. About five seconds later, we fall from the tunnel into an open area. The walls are lined with folds. As more and more material falls upon and around us, the folds expand and smooth out. An acid liquid, as well as a lubricating liquid, are added to our mixture by cells in the walls. Soon everything around us has changed into a thin, watery liquid.

We are moved to a small tube, and begin traveling through it. The walls have many ridges and folds and are covered by tiny fingers of tissue. Juices are added, including a greenish fluid. We continue to be bathed by a soupy liquid. Then we stop. The liquid begins to absorb into the walls and move out into the rest of the body.

We have experienced what it is like to be digested. **Digestion** is the process that breaks down food into smaller molecules so they can move into the blood. Food is processed in the digestive system for the purpose of supplying the body with nutrients. What is not digested is eliminated.

The human digestive system can be described as a tube divided into several specialized sections: mouth, esophagus, stomach, small intestine, large intestine, rectum, and anus. Food passes through all of these organs. However, also included in the digestive system are the liver, pancreas, and gall bladder. These organs produce enzymes and chemicals that help digest food, but food does not pass through them. **Enzymes** are molecules of proteins that speed up the chemical reactions in your body.

Let's review the journey we took through the body. Digestion begins in your mouth, where tongue and teeth break food up into small pieces. **Saliva,** a watery substance that contains mucus and an enzyme, helps to soften the food. The food then travels through the **esophagus,** a muscular tube about 25 centimeters long, and into the stomach. This process takes about four to ten seconds.

Your stomach is covered with folds, and as food enters, the stomach expands, smoothing out the folds. Here, food is mixed by the muscular walls of the stomach with strong digestive juices that include an acid and enzymes. This process takes about four hours.

Digestive System

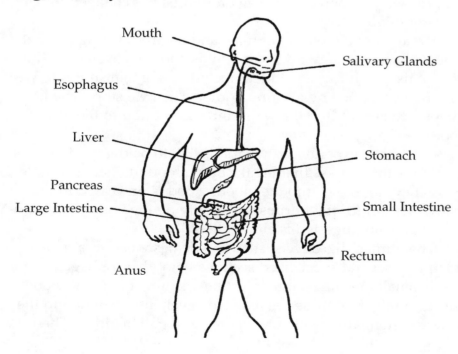

When this part of the process is completed, the food has changed to a thin, watery liquid called **chyme.** Chyme moves into the small intestine, which is about four to seven meters long! Here digestive juices from the pancreas and liver are added. Your liver produces a greenish fluid called **bile,** which is stored in a small sac called the gall bladder. Bile breaks up large particles of fat.

At this time, chyme is absorbed by the body. Blood transports the nutrients to all the cells of the body. The remaining materials are absorbed into the large intestine. The large intestine absorbs water from the undigested mass, and returns the water to the body. Chyme may stay here for as long as three days. The remaining undigested materials become more solid. Muscles in the rectum and anus will expel the solid wastes from the body.

Look at the diagram of the digestive system on the previous page. After you have memorized the major parts, test yourself on the blank diagram below.

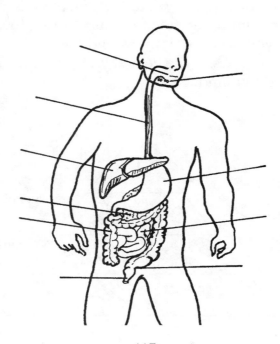

Health Note: The purpose of your digestive system is to break down food so that your body is supplied with nutrients. **Nutrients** are substances in foods that provide energy. What happens if much of the food you eat is poor in nutrients? Your body will go through the process of breaking down what you have eaten without receiving any beneficial nutrients.

It is important to eat foods that are rich in nutrients so that your body can provide you with the energy you need for the many activities in which you participate. Because no one food has every nutrient, you need to eat a variety of foods. Foods that contain the same nutrients belong to a food group. It is important to eat foods from each food group every day. Eating a certain amount from each food group every day will supply your body with the nutrients it needs for energy and growth.

Look at the food pyramid below. Write down everything you eat today. Tomorrow, analyze today's diet to see if you have eaten the right amounts of each food group. Write down the food groups in which you need to eat more, and the food groups in which you need to eat less. The next day, adjust your diet so that it follows the food pyramid.

Food Pyramid

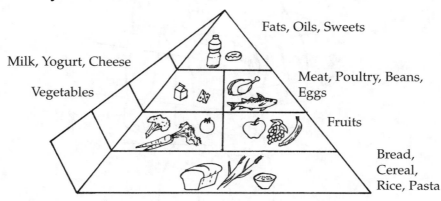

Fats, Oils, Sweets

Milk, Yogurt, Cheese

Vegetables

Meat, Poultry, Beans, Eggs

Fruits

Bread, Cereal, Rice, Pasta

Chapter 14 Review

1. What is the body's largest organ?

2. Name three functions of the skin.

3. When should you see a doctor about a mole on your skin?

4. Compare the central and peripheral nervous systems.

5. Define sensory neurons, interneurons, and motor neurons.

6. A small spaces between neurons that an impulse moves across is called a _____.

7. Name the five senses.

8. Define olfactory cells and taste buds.

9. Describe how taste buds are arranged on your tongue.

10. Name one drug that affects your nervous system and explain how it affects it.

11. Compare voluntary and involuntary muscles and give an example of each.

12. Name the three types of muscles and their functions.

13. What happens to muscles that are not exercised?

14. Define cardiovascular system.

15) Compare arteries and veins.

16. How can a person prevent heart disease?

17. Name two functions of the skeletal system.

18. What are two causes of osteoporosis?

19. Describe one lung disease that can be directly related to smoking.

20. Define enzymes and saliva.

21. What other organs, through which food does not pass, help with the digestive process?

22. Define nutrients.

23. Create a sample menu for a person your age that includes all the proper amounts of food that should be eaten, as given in the food pyramid.

PERIODIC TABLE OF THE ELEMENTS

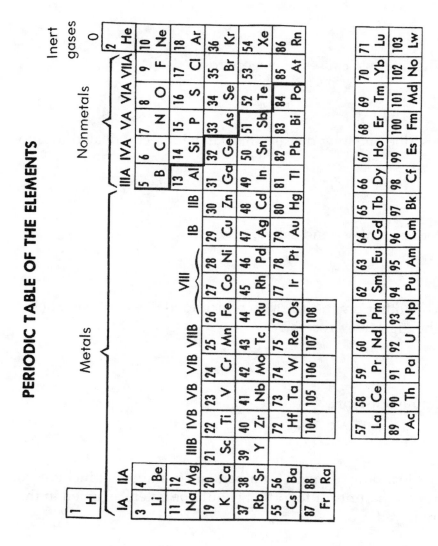

GLOSSARY

A

abyssal plain: large flat area on the ocean floor

abyssal zone: open ocean zone that extends from an average depth of 2000 meters to approximately 6000 meters

air mass: a large body of air that has taken on the properties of the land it covers

air pressure: the force of air pressing down on the earth's surface

amphibian: ectothermic vertebrate that spends part of its life in water and part of its life on land

anemometer: instrument used to measure wind speed

angiosperm: a flower-producing, vascular, seed-producing plant

anus: an opening at the end of the digestive system through which waste leaves the body

artery: a vessel that moves blood away from the heart

asteroid belt: a ring of asteroids that sweeps around the sun, found between the orbits of Mars and Jupiter

asthenosphere: the layer of the earth found between the lithosphere and mantle

astronomy: the study of the planets, stars, and other objects found in space

atmosphere: a mixture of gases that surround the earth

atherosclerosis: a disorder in which blood flow is restricted by fatty deposits that have formed on artery walls

autumnal equinox: the fall time of year in which the day and night are of equal length; marks the beginning of autumn for the Northern Hemisphere

axis: an imaginary vertical line around which a body spins or rotates

axon: the part of a neuron that carries messages away from the cell body

B

barometer: an instrument used to measure air pressure

bathyal zone: open-ocean zone that extends from a continental slope down approximately 2000 meters

bedrock: layer of rock beneath the soil

benthos: organisms that live on the ocean floor

bilateral symmetry: describes animals with body parts arranged the same on both sides of the body

binary star: a double-star system

biosphere: all parts of the earth where life exists

C

caldera: large crater formed when the sides of a volcanic cone collapse

capillary: a microscopic blood vessel through which nutrients, oxygen, and wastes pass

cardiac muscle: involuntary muscle tissue found only in the heart

carnivore: an animal that eats only other animals

cartilage: a tough, flexible tissue that covers the ends of bones to allow movement

cell: the smallest unit of life

cell membrane: the outer boundary of a cell

cell wall: the rigid structure of cellulose that surrounds a plant cell

central nervous system: the brain and the spinal cord

chloroplasts: plant cell organelles in which light energy is converted into chemical energy

chromosphere: the middle layer of the sun's atmosphere

chyme: the thin, watery liquid in the digestive tract

class: the classification group below phylum

cleavage: a mineral's tendency to break along smooth, definite surfaces

climate: the average weather conditions of an area over a long period of time

cnidarian: a phylum of animals with stinging cells

coma: the cloud that surrounds the nucleus of a comet

comet: an object made of ice, gas, and dust that orbits the sun periodically

community: all the populations of different species that live in the same place at the same time and interact with each other

composition: the materials of which an object or organism is made

compound: the chemical substance made from different elements that are bonded together by the sharing, giving away, or taking of atoms

compression: type of stress on the earth's crust that squeezes rocks together

condensation: a stage in the water cycle in which water vapor changes back into a liquid

conifer: needle-leafed tree that produces its seeds in cones

constellation: a group of stars in which people have seen imaginary people or animals

consumers: organisms that cannot make their own food

continent: a major land mass that measures millions of square kilometers and rises a considerable distance above sea level

continental glacier: a thick sheet of snow and ice that covers thousands of square kilometers and moves slowly in different directions

continental shelf: the gradually sloping end of every continent that extends out under the ocean

continental slope: a part of the continental shelf that dips steeply down to the ocean floor

coral reef: a large mass of limestone rocks found in tropical waters that surround an island

core: the center of an object such as the sun or the earth

corona: the outermost layer of the sun's atmosphere

crater: the pit at the top of a volcanic cone

crest: the highest point of a wave

crust: the thin, rocky, outer layer of the earth

crystal: a solid in which the atoms or molecules are arranged in a definite pattern that repeats itself

cytoplasm: the gel-like substance inside the cell membrane

D

data: recorded measurements and observations

day: the time it takes for a planet to rotate 360 degrees.

deep current: ocean current deep in the ocean caused by the differences in the density of the water

deep zone: extremely cold and high pressure region of water below the thermocline

deformation: any geological change in the original shape or volume of rocks

dendrite: the part of the nerve cell which receives messages and sends them to the cell body

dermis: the inner layer of skin

diameter: the width of an object

digestion: the process that breaks down food into small molecules to be used by the organism

division: the second highest classification group in plants

double planet: two planets that revolve around each other

E

Earth: the third planet from the sun

earthquake: the sudden movement of part of the earth's crust

echinoderm: ocean invertebrate with spiny skin that moves by means of a water-vascular system

ecology: the study of relationships between organisms and between organisms and their physical environments

ecosystem: a community interacting with the nonliving parts of its environment

ectotherm: vertebrate animal whose internal body temperature changes with its environment

element: a substance that cannot be separated into simpler substances by ordinary chemical means

elevation: height above sea level

elliptical galaxy: a type of galaxy that has a nearly spherical or flat shape

endoplasmic reticulum: a cell organelle that moves materials in the cell

endotherm: vertebrate animal that maintains a constant body temperature

enzyme: a protein that speeds chemical reactions

epidermis: the surface or outer layer of the skin

equator: the imaginary line around the fattest part of the earth

erosion: the movement of weathered substances

escape velocity: the velocity necessary to escape the earth's gravitational pull

estivation: an animal's period of inactivity in response to extremely hot conditions

evaporation: the process by which liquid is turned into water vapor

exoskeleton: the hard, lightweight external covering of arthropods that supports and protects the body

exosphere: the upper part of the thermosphere

F

fault: a break or crack in the crust of the earth

filter feeder: an organism that obtains food by filtering it from the water in which it lives

fish: an ectothermic vertebrate with gills, fins, and scales that lives in water

fold: a bend in rock

fracture: the way a mineral breaks along a rough or jagged surface

free-living: an organism that does not depend on any one organism for its food and place to live

front: the boundary where two air masses meet

G

galaxy: a huge collection of stars

giant star: a star with a diameter that is 10 to 100 times larger than the sun

glacier: a large mass of moving ice or snow

globe: a round model of the earth

golgi bodies: cell organelles that package and move proteins to the outside of the cell

gravity: the force of attraction between objects

groundwater: water that soaks into the ground and remains there

guyot: a sea mount in which the top has been broken off and is submerged

gymnosperm: a vascular plant that produces its seeds in cones

H

hardness: the ability of a mineral to resist being scratched

hemisphere: the halves of the earth divided by the equator

herbivore: an animal that eats only plants

hibernation: an animal's period of inactivity in response to extreme cold

highlands: the moon's mountain ranges

horizon: a soil layer

humus: decayed organic material

hydrosphere: the water-covered part of the earth's surface

I

iceberg: a large chunk of ice that breaks off a continental glacier and drifts out to sea

igneous rock: rock formed from lava or magma that has cooled

impermeable layer: layer of material through which water cannot move

inertia: the tendency of matter to remain at rest or continue in the same direction and at the same rate unless acted upon by some outside force (such as gravity)

inner core: the solid, innermost center of the earth

inner planets: Mercury, Venus, Earth, and Mars

inorganic: matter that is not formed from living things or the remains of living things

international date line: the line located at the 180th meridian; a day is added when the line is crossed going west; a day is subtracted when the line is crossed going east.

interneurons: nerve cells that transmit impulses from sensory neurons to motor neurons

intertidal zone: the region between the low and high tide

invertebrate: an animal without a backbone

involuntary muscle: a muscle that cannot be consciously controlled

ion: an electrically charged particle

ionosphere: the lower part of the thermosphere

isostasy: the balance formed by the downward force of the earth's crust and the upward force of the earth's mantle

irregular galaxy: a galaxy that has neither a spiral nor an elliptical shape

J

jet stream: strong winds that blow horizontally around a planet

joint: any place where two bones meet

Jupiter: the fifth planet from the sun

L

land breeze: wind that flows from land to sea

landscape: the physical features of the earth's surface in a region

latitude: the measure of distance north and south of the equator

lava: molten rock at the earth's surface

light-year: the distance light travels in a year

lithosphere: the topmost solid layer of the earth

longitude: the measure of distance east and west of the prime meridian

long-period comet: a comet that returns to the sun over a period of thousands of years

luster: the way in which a mineral's surface reflects light

lysosome: a cell organelle that digests wastes and worn-out cell parts

M

magma: molten rock beneath the earth's surface

magnetosphere: the area around a planet in which the planet's magnetic force operates

mammal: an endothermic vertebrate with hair that produces milk for its young

mantle: the layer of the earth between the crust and the outer core

map: a drawing of the earth or a part of the earth's surface

maria: the moon's smooth, lowland plains

marrow: fatty tissue in bone that produces red and white blood cells

Mars: the fourth planet from the sun

marsupial: a mammal with a pouch on its abdomen for carrying and nursing its young

matter: anything that takes up space and has mass

medium-sized star: a star that varies from about one-tenth the size of the sun to about ten times the size of the sun

Mercury: the planet closest to the sun

meridian: a line that runs between the North and South Poles

mesosphere: the layer of the earth's atmosphere between the thermosphere and stratosphere

metamorphic rock: rock changed by heat, pressure and/or chemical reactions

metamorphosis: a series of changes in the form of a body during the life cycle

meteor: a streak of light produced by a meteoroid as it burns up in the earth's atmosphere

meteorite: a meteor that strikes the Earth's surface

meteoroid: chunk of metal or stone that orbits the sun

meteorologist: a scientist who studies the earth's atmosphere, weather, and climate

mid-ocean ridge: a mountain chain beneath the ocean where new ocean floor is produced

mineral: a naturally occurring, inorganic solid that has a definite chemical composition and crystal shape

minor planets: the asteroids found in the asteroid belt between the orbits of Mars and Jupiter

mitochondria: a cell organelle that breaks down food molecules and releases energy

mixture: two or more substances physically combined

molecule: two or more atoms held together by a chemical bond

mollusk: a soft-bodied invertebrate that usually has a hard shell

monotreme: a mammal that lays eggs having tough, leathery shells

motor neuron: nerve cell that conducts impulses from the brain or spinal cord to muscles or glands in the body

mountain: a natural raised part of the earth that has high elevations, steep sides, and a narrow summit

multiple-star system: a group of two or more stars that revolve around each other

muscle: an organ that relaxes and contracts to allow movement

N

neap tide: a tide that is lower than usual because the sun interferes with the moon's gravitational pull

nekton: ocean life forms that swim

Neptune: the eighth planet from the sun

neritic zone: the area of the ocean that extends from the low-tide line to the edge of a continental shelf

neuron: a nerve cell that carries impulses throughout the body

neutron star: the smallest of all types of stars

night: the time during which a side of a revolving body is facing away from the sun

nonvascular plant: a plant without vascular tissue that absorbs water directly through its cell membranes

nucleus: the structure inside a cell that controls the cell's activities; the center of an atom; the core of a comet

nutrient: a substance in food that produces energy and materials for life activities

O

oceanographer: a scientist who studies the ocean

olfactory cells: nerve cells in nasal passages that help an organism to smell

omnivore: an animal that eats both plants and animals

orbit: the path of an object revolving around another object in space

organelles: the structures within eukaryotic cells that perform various functions for the cell

osteoporosis: a disease that breaks down bone, making it brittle and weak

outer core: the layer of the earth between the inner core and the mantle

outer planets: Jupiter, Saturn, Uranus, Neptune, and Pluto

ozone: the gas in the earth's atmosphere that shields the earth from harmful ultraviolet rays

P

parallel: a line going from east to west across a map or globe that is parallel to the equator

parasite: an organism that depends on another organism for its food and a place to live

period of revolution: the time it takes for a planet to make one revolution around the sun

period of rotation: the time it takes for a planet to complete one rotation on its axis

periosteum: a tough, tight-fitting membrane that covers the surface of bones

peripheral nervous system: the part of the nervous system that connects the brain and spinal cord to other body parts

permeable layer: a layer of material through which water can move quickly

pharynx: a tubelike passageway for both food and air

photosphere: the innermost layer of the sun's atmosphere

photosynthesis: a plant function that converts light energy into chemical energy

phylum: the second category in the classification of animals

placenta: the sack-like organ that surrounds an embryo and absorbs food and oxygen from the mother through the blood

placental mammal: a mammal whose young develop inside the female in the uterus

plain: a flat land area that does not rise far above sea level

plankton: animals and plants that float at or near the ocean's surface

plateau: a flat land area that rises high above sea level

Pluto: the planet furthest from the sun

polar zone: the climate zone extending from the pole (90 degrees) to about 60 degrees latitude in each hemisphere

pollen grain: the male reproductive part of a plant that contains the sperm

pollination: the process that transfers pollen grains to the egg cell in a plant

population: organisms of one species that live in the same place at the same time and that can produce offspring

precipitation: the stage in the water cycle in which the water falls to the earth in the form of rain, snow, sleet, or hail

prime meridian: the 0-degree and 180-degree meridian

producer: an organism that can make its own food

R

radial symmetry: describes animals with body parts arranged around a central point

rain gauge: an instrument used to measure rainfall

regeneration: the ability of an organism to grow new body parts

relief: the difference in a region's elevations

reptile: an ectothermic vertebrate that has dry, scaly skin and that lays eggs covered with a leathery shell

reservoir: an man-made lake used as a source of fresh water

residual soil: the soil that remains on the top of the rock from which it was formed

respiration: the process by which organisms break down food to release energy

retrograde rotation: the rotation of a planet from east to west, instead of west to east

Richter scale: the scale used to measure the strength of earthquakes

rille: a moon valley

rock: a hard substance formed by the mixture of one or more minerals

rock cycle: the continuous process of rocks changing from one kind to another

S

saliva: the watery substance produced in the mouth that begins the chemical digestion of food

Saturn: the sixth planet from the sun

scale: the relationship between the distances on the earth and the distances used on a map

scales: hard, thin, overlapping plates that cover and protect a fish's body

sea breeze: a wind that flows from the sea to the land

sea mount: a volcanic mountain on the ocean floor

sedimentary rock: rock that is formed by the compacting or cementing of sediments

seismograph: an instrument used to record seismic waves produced by earthquakes

sensory neuron: nerve cell that transmits messages to the brain or spinal cord

shearing: type of stress on the earth's crust that pushes rock in opposing horizontal directions

short-period comet: a comet that returns to the sun over a period of a few years

skeletal muscles: voluntary muscles that move bones

smooth muscles: involuntary muscles that move many internal organs

solar system: the sun, planets, and all the other objects that revolve around the sun

spiral galaxy: a galaxy that is shaped like a pinwheel

spontaneous generation: the theory that nonliving things produce living things

spring tide: a higher than usual tide that results from the additional gravitational pull of the sun

stratosphere: the layer of the earth between earth's troposphere and the mesosphere

streak: the color of powder left by a mineral when it is rubbed against a hard, rough surface

stress: the pushing, pulling and twisting of the earth's crust

subsoil: the layer of soil above bedrock, and, in mature soil, below the layer of topsoil

summer solstice: the time of year when the Northern Hemisphere has its longest day, and the Southern Hemisphere has its shortest day; marks the beginning of summer for the Northern Hemisphere

supergiant stars: the largest of all stars; a star with a diameter up to 1000 times the diameter of the sun

superheated water: water that is under so much pressure and heat that it does not evaporate

surface current: an ocean current at the surface that is moved mainly by winds

synapse: the small gap between two neurons

T

taste buds: taste receptors located on the tongue that allow an organism to taste

temperate zone: the climate zone located between 60 degrees and 30 degrees latitude in each hemisphere

thermocline: the zone in which the temperature of ocean water drops rapidly

thermometer: an instrument used to measure temperature

thermosphere: the outer layer of the earth's atmosphere; the thermosphere is divided into the ionosphere and the exosphere

tide: the rise and fall of the earth's oceans which is caused by the moon's gravitational pull on the Earth

time zone: the region of Earth where all areas have the same local time

topography: the shape of the Earth's surface

topsoil: the uppermost layer of mature soil

transpiration: the phase in the water cycle in which water vapor evaporates from plants, animals and the land

trench: a deep valley located around the edges of the ocean floor

tropical zone: the climate zone located between 30 degrees latitude and the equator in each hemisphere

troposphere: the innermost layer of the earth's atmosphere

trough: the lowest point of a wave

tsunami: a giant ocean wave produced by an earthquake

U

upwelling: the rising of deep, cold currents to the ocean surface

Uranus: the seventh planet from the sun

V

valley glacier: a long, narrow glacier that moves down a mountain valley

vascular plant: a plant containing vascular tissue that transports food and water through the plant

vein: a vessel that moves blood toward the heart

vent: an opening through which lava erupts

Venus: the second planet from the sun

vernal equinox: the spring time of year when day and night are of equal length; marks the beginning of spring for the Northern Hemisphere

vertebrate: an animal with a backbone

volcano: a place where molten rock and other materials reach the earth's surface

voluntary muscle: a muscle that can be consciously controlled

W

water cycle: the continuous movement of water from the oceans and freshwater sources to the air and land and back to the oceans

water table: the level that marks where the ground below it is saturated with water

water-vascular system: an echinoderm's network of water-filled canals to which thousands of tube feet are connected, allowing the animal to move and eat

wavelength: the horizontal distance between two crests or troughs

weathering: the process by which rocks and other materials are broken down

white dwarf: a small, dense star that is larger than a neutron star, but smaller than a medium-sized star

winter solstice: the time of year when the Northern Hemisphere has its shortest day, and the Southern Hemisphere has its longest day; marks the beginning of winter for the Northern Hemisphere

Z

zone of aeration: the region underground in which the spaces between the rocks and particles of soil are filled with air
zone of saturation: the region underground in which the spaces between the rocks and particles of soil are filled with water

ANSWER
KEY

Answers to Chapter 1 Review Questions

1. A mixture of gases surrounding a star or planet.
2. Very hot gases.
3. The corona (outer layer of sun's atmosphere), chromosphere (middle layer of sun's atmosphere), photosphere (inner layer of sun's atmosphere), and core (sun's center).
4. The photosphere is the brightest layer of the sun. The core is the hottest part of the sun.
5. A model is a three-dimensional representation of an object.
6. Inner planets: Mercury, Venus, Earth, and Mars; outer planets: Jupiter, Saturn, Uranus, Neptune, and Pluto.
7. The asteroid belt that sweeps around the sun between the orbits of Mars and Jupiter.
8. Venus rotates in a retrograde motion.
9. Answers will vary. Some main characteristics may include that Earth has life, a rocky crust, and a hydrosphere.
10. Martian soil is made of the chemical iron oxide, or rust, and gives the planet a red color.
11. Pluto; Jupiter.
12. Gas giants.
13. Saturn.
14. Uranus and Neptune.
15. Pluto and its moon, Charon.
16. A vast collection of ice, gas and dust about 15 trillion kilometers from the sun.
17. Long-period comets may take thousands of years to orbit the sun again. Short-period comets orbit the sun every few years.
18. A meteorite.

Answers to Chapter 2 Review Questions:

1. Alpha Centauri.
2. Navigation, timing of crops, for signs.
3. According to size, composition, surface temperature, and color.
4. Constellations are groups of stars in which people at one time saw imaginary figures of animals and people. Answers will vary.
5. Shapley and Kant. Kant. Answers will vary. Kant believed there were many galaxies.

Answers to Chapter 3 Review Questions:

1. Overcoming gravity.
2. Fasten everything down to keep things from floating away, food must be squeezed from tubes, and special exercises.
3. Answers will vary.

Matching:
1. Tsiolkovsky
2. Newton
3. Wernher von Braun
4. Armstrong and Aldrin
5. Goddard

Answers to Chapter 4 Review Questions:

1. The extreme, hot temperature, and high pressure and density make it difficult to study.
2. The mantle contains 80 percent of Earth's volume and 68 percent of Earth's mass.
3. When a solid has the ability to flow.
4. Because of the enormous pressure at this depth, elements remain solid.

Answers to Chapter 5 Review Questions

1. Igneous rock is formed by cooled magma; sedimentary rock is formed by layers of rocks and sand pressed and cemented together over time; and metamorphic rock is formed by igneous and/or sedimentary rock being changed by heat, pressure, and chemical action.
2. The earth's crust has an average thickness of eight kilometers.
3. The shaking and trembling that results from the sudden movement of part of the Earth's crust. Scientists study earthquakes by studying seismic waves. They measure seismic waves with a seismograph, using the Richter scale to measure the strength of an earthquake.
4. A break in the earth's crust
5. Magma is liquid rock under the earth's surface. Lava is liquid rock at the earth's surface.
6. A crater is a pit at the top of a volcanic cone. A caldera is a crater that is formed when the walls of the volcanic cone collapse.
7. An active volcano is one that erupts continually or periodically. A dormant volcano has erupted in modern times, but is now inactive. An extinct volcano has not erupted within modern times.
8. Compression moves rocks of the crust closer together. Tension pulls rocks of the crust apart. Shearing pushes rocks of the crust in opposite, horizontal directions.
9. A fault is a crack in the earth's crust by which rocks move past one another. A fold is a bend in rock.
10. The balance between the upward pressure of the mantle and the downward pressure of the earth's crust.

Answers to Chapter 6 Review Questions:

1. Antarctica, Australia, Asia, Africa, North America, South America, and Europe.
2. A land mass measuring millions of square kilometers and rising far above sea level.
3. Asia, Africa, and Europe.
4. Answers will vary.
5. Topography is the shape of the earth's surface. A landscape is a physical feature of the Earth's surface found in an area.
6. A map is a drawing or picture of earth on a flat surface. A model is three-dimensional representation of a larger object. A globe is the most accurate representation of the earth because it shows the true shape and location of Earth's land masses.
7. Meridians are lines running from the North and South Poles. Longitude measures the distances east and west of meridians.
8. The prime meridian.
9. Answer will vary.
10. Parallels are lines on a map or a globe that run from east to west and parallel the equator. Latitude is the measure of distance north and south of the equator.
11. The equator.

Answers to Chapter 7 Review Questions:

1. Answers will vary.
2. Answers will vary. Answers may include survival, recreation, or power.
3. Answers will vary.
4. Approximately 75 percent.
5. Approximately 97 percent. Approximately 3 percent.
6. Answers will vary.
7. Answers will vary. Answers should include the following defi-

nitions and stages: 1) Evaporation causes the water to change from the liquid phase to the gas phase. Only pure, fresh water is lifted into the air. 2) Condensation is the process by which water vapor changes back to a liquid. 3) Precipitation is the process by which water falls to the Earth.

8. A valley glacier is a long, narrow glacier that moves down mountain valleys. A continental glacier extends millions of square kilometers, is several thousand meters thick, and moves slowly in all directions.

9. Large chunks of ice that break off from glaciers and drift into the sea.

10. Lakes, ponds, and reservoirs.

11. Pacific, Atlantic, and Indian.

12. A sea is a part of an ocean that is nearly surrounded by land.

13. Oceanographers.

14. Answers will vary. Answers should include that surface currents are caused by wind patterns and have a depth of several hundred meters, and deep currents are caused by the differences in the density of water and usually flow in the opposite direction of surface currents.

15. Matching: 1. trench 2. seamount 3. coral reef 4. mid-ocean ridge 5. rift valley 6. guyot 7. abyssal plains.

Answers to Chapter 8 Review Questions

1. A mixture of gases that surround the earth.
2. The stratosphere.
3. A shield against the sun's harmful ultraviolet radiation.
4. It protects the earth from meteoroids.
5. The ionosphere and exonosphere are the lower and upper parts of the thermosphere. Answers will vary.
6. Weather is the daily condition of the atmosphere.
7. Heat, winds, and moisture.

8. The sun.

9. Winds are formed by the movement of air from one place to another. Warm air rises and cooler air moves under the rising warm air.

10. Rain, sleet, snow, or hail.

11. Air masses are large bodies of air that has taken on the temperature and humidity of a part of the earth's surface. A polar front is the boundary where cold air meets warm air.

12. Answers will vary.

13. Climate is the average weather at a particular place. Tropical, polar, and temperate.

14. Answers will vary.

Answers to Chapter 9 Review Questions

1. A body moving in orbit around a larger body.

2. The moon.

3. Waxing is the process by which the moon becomes more lighted. Waning is the process by which the moon becomes more darkened.

4. The moon is 384,403 kilometers away from the earth.

5. The moon's marias are broad, smooth, lowland plains. Its highlands are mountain ranges that reach eight kilometers above the surrounding plains. Its rilles are long valleys that crisscross the surface of the moon.

6. Tides occur because of the gravitational pull of the moon on the earth.

Answers to Chapter 10 Review Questions:

1. Matter is anything that takes up space and has mass. The three forms of matter are elements, compounds, and mixtures.

2. Answers will vary.

3. A compound is made of different elements that are chemically bonded together. A mixture is two or more substances mixed together, but each substance retains its own properties.
4. A molecule is two or more atoms held together by chemical forces.
5. Units.
6. Cell membrane, cytoplasm, and nucleus.
7. Eukaryotic cell are more complex. They have membrane bound organelles, and a nucleus with a membrane. Prokaryotic cells have no organelles and nuclear material that has no membrane.
8. Answers will vary.
9. All cells come from cells that already exist.
10. Matching: 1. J 2. I 3. C 4. G 5. H 6. A 7. E 8. F 9. D 10. B

Answers to Chapter 11 Review Questions:

1. Naturally occurring, inorganic, solid, crystal structure, and chemical composition.
2. Answers will vary.
3. A rock is a hard substance that is usually made up of two or more minerals mixed together.
4. Weathering is a process that breaks rocks into smaller pieces. Erosion is a process by which soil and weathered rocks are moved. Compaction is the process that presses layers and layers of sediments deposited by erosion together. Cementation is the process that presses together large sediments, using water to dissolve minerals and cement the sediments together.
5. Pieces of weathered rock and organic material.
6. Residual remains above the bedrock from which it was formed. Transported soil is moved away by water, wind, glaciers, and waves.
7. Answers will vary. Answers should include that topsoil is a dark-colored soil layer in which much activity by living organisms

takes place; subsoil is made of clay, humus, and perhaps some minerals that have been washed down from the topsoil.

Answers to Chapter 12 Review Questions

1. Answers may vary. Answers should include that seedless plants grow from spores; seed plants grow from seeds.
2. Vascular tissue transports nutrients through the plant.
3. Examples may include mosses and liverworts; club mosses and spike mosses; horsetails; and ferns.
4. Answers will vary.
5. Answers will vary. Examples may include construction, paper, chemicals for soap, paint, and varnish.
6. A body produced by angiosperms containing seeds.
7. Answers will vary.
8. Leaves, stems, and roots. Descriptions will vary.
9. The process by which plants and animals create offspring.
10. Seeds store food for plant embryos to grow when conditions are favorable.
11. Pollination.
12. Answers will vary.

Answers to Chapter 13 Review Questions

1. Water animals and birds first, then land animals.
2. Both animals and plants have many cells, and those cells are eukaryotic.
3. Invertebrates do not have a backbone; vertebrates do.
4. Animals with body parts arranged the same way on both sides have bilateral symmetry. Animals with body parts arranged around a central point have radial symmetry. Animals with no definite arrangement of body parts have asymmetry.

5. A filter feeder filters its food out of the water.

6. "Cnidaria" is Latin for "stinging cells."

7. A parasite is an animal that depends on another animal, its host, for food and a place to live. A free-living organism does not depend on one particular organism for food or a place to live.

8. Heartworm.

9. Gastropods, bivalves, and cephalopods. Descriptions will vary.

10. "Annelid" means "little rings." Answers will vary.

11. Exoskeleton is an external covering that covers, supports and protects the body. Arthropods.

12. Regeneration is the ability of an animal to grow new body parts. Answers will vary. Examples may include arthropods and echinoderms.

13. The water vascular system is a unique network of water-filled canals. Water moves into and out of the system through tube feet that act as suction cups, helping the animal to move and feed.

14. Ectotherms are animals in which their internal body temperatures change with the temperature of their surroundings. Endotherms have a constant body temperature.

15. Jawless, cartilaginous, and bony fish.

16. "Double life." Because amphibians live part of their lives in water and part on land.

17. Hibernation is a period of inactivity in response to extreme cold. Estivation is a period of inactivity in response to extreme heat.

18. They do not need water to reproduce.

19. Lizards have moveable eyelids, external ears, and legs with clawed toes on each foot. Snakes do not have legs, eyelids, or external ears.

20. Answers will vary. Examples may include that birds have two wings, feathers, and lay eggs with a hard shell.

21. Answers will vary. Examples may include that mammals are endotherms, nurse their young, have skin and hair on their bodies.

22. Mammals produce milk to feed their young.
23. Answers will vary. Examples may include the duckbilled platypus (monotreme), kangaroo (marsupial), and human (placental).

Answers to Chapter 14 Review Questions:

1. The skin
2. Protects the body; allows our bodies to sense temperature, pressure and pain; and helps to regulate body temperature.
3. When new moles appear or there is a change in color, shape, or size of existing moles.
4. The central nervous system consists of the brain and the spinal cord. The peripheral nervous system includes all the nerves outside of the central nervous system.
5. Sensory neurons receive information and send impulses to the brain or spinal cord. Interneurons relay impulses from the sensory to motor neurons. Motor neurons conduct impulses from the brain or spinal cord to muscles or glands throughout the body.
6. Synapses.
7. Sight, smell, taste, touch, and hearing.
8. Olfactory cells are nerve cells in the nasal passages that help a person to smell. Taste buds are the sensory receptors on the tongue that allow a person to taste.
9. Sweet is tasted at the tip of the tongue. Salty and sour are tasted in the middle of the tongue. Bitter is tasted at the back of the tongue.
10. Answers will vary.
11. Voluntary muscles are muscles a person can control. Involuntary muscles are muscles that move and work without a person controlling their motions.
12. Skeletal muscles move bones. Smooth muscles many internal organs. Cardiac muscle makes up the heart.
13. They become smaller in size.

14. Cardiovascular system is a bodily system which includes the heart, blood, and blood vessels, and functions to circulate blood throughout the body.

15. Answers will vary. Answers should include that arteries carry blood away from the heart; veins carry blood to the heart.

16. Answers will vary.

17. Answers will vary. Examples may include giving shape and support to the body, protecting internal organs, or storing calcium and phosphorous.

18. Answers will vary. Examples may include a diet low in calcium, consuming too much caffeine, and getting too little exercise.

19. Answers will vary.

20. Enzymes are molecules of proteins that speed up the chemical reactions in the body. Saliva is a watery substance that contains mucus and an enzyme and helps to soften food.

21. Answers will vary. Examples may include liver, pancreas, or gall bladder.

22. Nutrients are substances in foods that provide energy.

23. Answers will vary.

Volume discounts of *How Does God Do That?* are available for wholesalers and home-school groups. For more information, please write to:

Coffee House Publishers,
32370 SE Judd Rd
Eagle Creek, Oregon 97022
503-637-3277 • coffeebooks@integrityonline.com
www.roadsearching.com

Speaking engagements for Paul and Danielle Harris are handled through the publisher. Please write or call to request a speakers packet.

Paul and Danielle Harris are starting a program that will teach biology and elements of science while hiking in the wilderness of the Oregon-Cascade mountain range. If you would like further information about this program, please contact the publisher.

For an interesting story on how Paul and Danielle met, consider reading *Prayer and the Art of Volkswagen Maintenance*. Yes, this is the same Paul and Danielle.